Study Guide

Ella Mae Matsumura

University of Wisconsin-Madison

S. Mark Young

University of Southern California

Second Edition

MANAGEMENT ACCOUNTING

Anthony A. Atkinson

Rajiv D. Banker

Robert S. Kaplan

S. Mark Young

PRENTICE HALL, Upper Saddle River, New Jersey 07458

Project Editor: *Joseph F. Tomasso*
Acquisitions Editor: *P. J. Boardman*
Assistant Editor: *Natacha St. Hill*
Manufacturing Buyer: *Paul Smolenski*

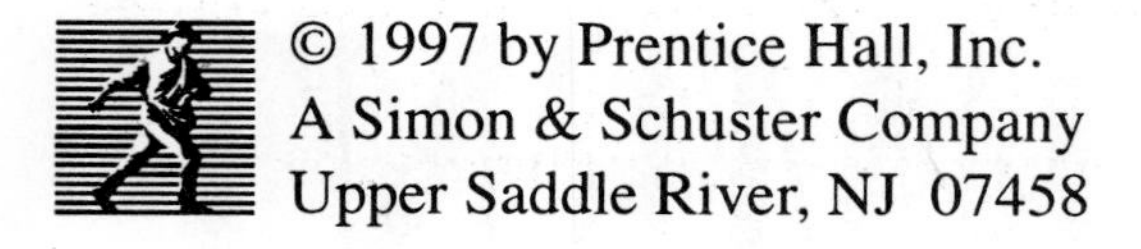

A Simon & Schuster Company
Upper Saddle River, NJ 07458

Printed in the United States of America

10 9 8 7 6 5 4 3 2

ISBN 0-13-262965-8

Prentice-Hall International (UK) Limited, *London*
Prentice-Hall of Australia Pty. Limited, *Sydney*
Prentice-Hall Canada Inc., *Toronto*
Prentice-Hall Hispanoamericana, S.A., *Mexico*
Prentice-Hall of India Private Limited, *New Delhi*
Prentice-Hall of Japan, Inc., *Tokyo*
Simon & Schuster Asia Pte. Ltd., *Singapore*
Editora Prentice-Hall do Brasil, Ltda., *Rio de Janiero*

Contents

To the Student

This study guide has been designed to accompany the second edition of Anthony A. Atkinson, Rajiv D. Banker, Robert S. Kaplan and S. Mark Young's textbook, *Management Accounting*. For each chapter, there is a corresponding Study Guide chapter that presents the central focus and objectives, a detailed review of key concepts, and a comprehensive set of practice test questions and problems.

Using the Textbook, Readings Book, and Study Guide

The textbook and book of readings are designed to provide students with state-of-the-art material on management accounting. The purpose of the Study Guide is to reinforce what you have learned, and even though it is quite detailed, *it is not a substitute for the textbook.* Although there are numerous ways to study this material, the following sequence can be very effective:

1. Read the entire chapter of the textbook to get an overview of the material.
2. Read the entire chapter again, this time taking notes, reflecting on the material and posing questions to yourself.
3. After you have studied the textbook, read the corresponding chapter in the Study Guide and compare your notes to the outlined material in the Guide.
   a. The *Review of Key Concepts* section is meant to be a *summary* of key terms and ideas.
   b. Pay particular attention to *check-marked boxes.* These boxes are designed to have you focus on particular exhibits in the text or key points to think about.
   c. The *Practice Test Questions and Problems* section is another opportunity to test your knowledge and ability with the material. Work these questions and problems *before* looking at the solutions!
   d. The *Notes and Questions* page at the end of each chapter provides a convenient place to make note of material to be clarified or important points to reinforce.
4. Work on the homework problems that your instructor has assigned. You will get the most benefit if you make a very strong initial attempt at the problems, ***on your own***. Working alone, to start, will tell you how well you have learned the material and will also help to develop your analytical and problem-solving skills.
5. If you have reached an impasse with the material and cannot solve some problems, then turn to the instructor or a friend for help.
6. Finally, after each class session, review the material again to reinforce what you have learned.

The area of management accounting has assumed a great deal of importance for managers and employees in all areas. Understanding this topic will help you tremendously in your careers, regardless of the path that you take. We hope that you enjoy the text and book of readings, and that you find the Study Guide helpful.

Ella Mae Matsumura
School of Business
University of Wisconsin-Madison

S. Mark Young
School of Accounting
University of Southern California

Acknowledgments

We would like to thank Natacha St. Hill, Assistant Editor, for her encouragement and editorial assistance with this edition of the Study Guide.

Chapter 1

Management Accounting:
Information That Creates Value

CENTRAL FOCUS AND LEARNING OBJECTIVES

After reading this chapter, you will be able to

1. appreciate the important role that management accounting information plays in both manufacturing and service organizations.

2. discuss the significant differences between management accounting and financial accounting.

3. understand how different people in the organization have different demands for management accounting information.

4. appreciate how management accounting creates value for organizations and how it relates to operations, marketing, and strategy.

5. explain why management accounting information must include both financial and nonfinancial information.

6. understand why activities should be the primary focus for measuring and managing performance in organizations.

7. discuss the role for multiple performance measures—financial and nonfinancial—to translate the organization's strategy into specific objectives and measures.

REVIEW OF KEY TERMS AND CONCEPTS

Learning Objective 1: Appreciate the important role that management accounting information plays in both manufacturing and service organizations.

I. The Role of Management Accounting in Organizations

A. A **management accounting system** is an information system that collects operational and financial data, processes it, stores it, and reports it to users such as workers, engineers, managers, and executives.

B. **Management accounting information** is output from a management accounting system (e.g., cost of a product, an activity, or a department).

C. **Management accounting** is the process of producing financial and operating information regarding the economic condition of the organization for users internal to the organization such as employees and managers. The process should be driven by the informational needs of individuals internal to the organization, and should guide their operating and investment decisions.

Learning Objective 2: Discuss the significant differences between management accounting and financial accounting.

D. In contrast, **financial accounting** differs from management accounting information, as financial accounting information and financial statements are produced for external constituencies, such as shareholders, creditors, and governmental authorities. This process is heavily constrained by standard-setting, regulatory, and tax authorities, and the auditing requirements of independent accountants (in contrast to management accounting).

Review textbook Exhibit 1-1.

Learning Objective 3:	Understand how different people in the organization have different demands for management accounting information.

Learning Objective 4:	Appreciate how management accounting creates value for organizations and how it relates to operations, marketing, and strategy.

Learning Objective 5:	Explain why management accounting information must include both financial and nonfinancial information.

II. Diversity of Management Accounting Information

Management accounting has many uses and can be widely diverse. Such information can include the quality of a service, quantitative inputs such as labor cost, profitability, efficiency, and capacity use.

A. **Strategic information** guides the long-term decision-making of the organization. Strategic information can include the profitability of products, services, and customers; competitors' behavior; customer preferences and trends; market opportunities and threats; and technological innovations.

1. **Critical success factors** are factors such as quality, on-time delivery, cost reduction, customer service, or product performance, that create long-term profitability for the organization.

2. **Benchmarking** is studying how other best-performing organizations, either internal or external to the firm, perform similar activities and processes.

B. Functions of Management Accounting Information

1. **Operational control** is the process of providing feedback to employees and their managers about the efficiency and quality of activities being performed.

2. **Product costing** is the process of measuring and assigning the costs of activities performed to design

and produce individual products (and services, for nonmanufacturing companies).

3. **Customer costing** is the process of assigning marketing, selling, distribution, and administrative costs to individual customers so that the cost of serving each customer can be calculated.

4. **Management control** is the process of providing information about the performance of managers and operating units.

5. **Strategic control** is the process of providing information about the organization's long-run competitive performance, market conditions, customer preferences, and technological innovations.

Be sure that you understand how the various functions of management accounting information differ.

III. Twentieth-Century Developments in Management Control.

A number of major innovations in management accounting occurred during the early part of the twentieth century.

A. At the Dupont Corporation these included developing:

1. An **operating budget**, which is a document that forecasts revenues and expenses during the next operating period, typically a year. The operating budget also authorizes spending on discretionary activities, such as research and development, advertising, maintenance, and employee training.

2. The **capital budget**, which is the management document that authorizes spending for resources, such as plant and equipment, that will have multiyear useful lifetimes.

3. The **return-on-investment formula**, which is the calculation that relates the profitability of an organizational unit to the investment required to

generate that profitability. The formula is often written as the return on sales (the ratio of operating income to sales) multiplied by the ratio of sales to assets employed (or investment).

$$\text{ROI} = \text{Operating Income/Investment}$$

$$= \text{Operating Income/Sales} \times \text{Sales/Investment}$$

B. At General Motors these included concepts such as:

1. **Decentralized responsibility**, which allows local division managers to make decisions on pricing, product mix, customer relationships, resource acquisition, materials sourcing, and operating processes without having to seek approval from higher-level managers. Decentralized responsibility also lets local managers make use of their superior access to information about local opportunities and threats.

2. **Centralized control**, which is the management process by which senior executives receive periodic information about decentralized divisional operations to assure that division managers are making decisions and taking actions that contribute to overall corporate goals.

3. A **flexible budget**, which is a forecast of what should have been given the actual volume and mix of production and sales.

IV. Comparing Service to Manufacturing Organizations

Service organizations:

A. Generally do not produce a product.

B. Have more direct contact with customers, so they must be very sensitive to timeliness and quality of service.

C. Have no inventory, per se.

D. Find it hard to control quality in advance, and thus defects are more likely and the consequences of poor service can be very strong.

Pick one manufacturing and one service organization with which you are familiar and compare them using points A-D preceding.

Learning Objective 6: Understand why activities should be the primary focus for measuring and managing performance in organizations.

V. Management Accounting Information in the Changing Competitive Environment

A. **Activity-based costing** is a procedure that measures the costs of objects such as products, services, and customers. Activity-based costing (ABC) first assigns resource costs to the activities performed by the organization. Then activity costs are assigned to products, customers, and services that benefit from or are creating the demand for activities.

B. **Activity-based management** is the management process that uses the information provided by an activity-based cost analysis to improve organizational profitability. Activity-based management (ABM) includes performing activities more efficiently, eliminating the need to perform certain activities that do not add value for customers, improving the design of products, and developing better relationships with customers and suppliers. The goal of ABM is to enable customer needs to be satisfied while making fewer demands on organizational resources.

C. **Continuous improvement** is the ongoing process by which employees continually problem-solve and search for methods to reduce and eliminate waste, improve quality and reduce defects, shorten response and cycle times, and design products that are simpler to manufacture, deliver, and service.

D. **Employee empowerment** is allowing employees who are closest to operating processes, customers, and suppliers to make decisions. Employees are encouraged to solve problems and devise creative new approaches for performing work and satisfying customers.

E. **Total quality** is a management philosophy that attempts to eliminate all defects, waste, and activities that do not add value to customers; also refers to an organizational commitment to customer satisfaction.

Learning Objective 7: Discuss the role for multiple performance measures—financial and nonfinancial—to translate the organization's strategy into specific objectives and measures.

F. The **Balanced Scorecard** is a multidimensional measurement system that translates an organization's mission and strategy into performance measures organized into four perspectives: financial, customer, internal business process, and learning and growth. The scorecard contains both outcome measures (such as return on investment and customer retention) and the performance drivers of those outcomes (such as motivated, skilled employees, high-quality and responsive production processes, and innovative products and services).

Review these key concepts; we will discuss them throughout the remaining chapters of the textbook.

PRACTICE TEST QUESTIONS AND PROBLEMS

True/False

__T__ 1. Management accounting information includes the cost and profitability of an organization's products, departments, services and activities.

__F__ 2. Management accounting information is generated primarily for use by constituencies external to the firm.

__F__ 3. Management accounting information is regulated by government authorities.

__T__ 4. Management accounting information encompasses operational and nonfinancial information.

__T__ 5. Companies have considerable choice in the design of their management accounting systems.

__T__ 6. Many of today's service and manufacturing organizations demand different and better management accounting information than in the early twentieth century.

__F__ 7. Functions are the central focus of the organization. (Activities -yes.)

__F__ 8. The term "flexible budget" means one that can be changed easily.

__T__ 9. Activity-based costing systems are designed to overcome cost distortions often introduced by traditional cost systems.

__T__ 10. The demand for management accounting information differs depending on the level of the organization.

Multiple-Choice

1. Management accounting information is developed for the following users, EXCEPT

   (a) shareholders.
   (b) middle managers.
   (c) senior executives.
   (d) operators/workers.

2. Which of the following answers best characterizes the role that management accounting information serves?

(a) Line control
(b) Span of control
(c) Management control
(d) Physical control

3. Critical success factors are variables that pertain

(a) only to short-term profitability of the firm.
(b) only to manufacturing organizations.
(c) only to service organizations.
(d) to the long-term profitability of the firm.

4. If operating income is $15,000, sales are $120,000, and investment is $300,000, return-on-investment is

(a) 12.5%.
(b) 5.0%.
(c) 40.0%.
(d) 250.0%.

5. At the heart of the Balanced Scorecard is a focus on

(a) business processes.
(b) checking that debits equal credits.
(c) ensuring that production workers have input into setting work standards.
(d) behavioral implications of management accounting information.

6. Customer costing is useful for determining

(a) the product cost that a customer expects.
(b) the product price that a customer expects.
(c) the cost of serving each customer.
(d) the total cost that a customer is willing to pay for products.

7. Flexible budgets take the following into account:

   (a) mix and growth of production and sales.
   (b) volume and growth of production and sales.
   (c) sales growth only.
   (d) volume and mix of production and sales.

8. Historically, service companies have used management accounting information

   (a) more intensively than manufacturing companies.
   (b) less intensively than manufacturing companies.
   (c) with the same intensity as manufacturing companies.
   (d) only for product costing.

9. The first step in using activity-based costing is to

   (a) assign activities to products.
   (b) assign resources to products.
   (c) assign resource costs to activities.
   (d) assign resource costs to products.

10. Each of the following is a goal of continuous improvement, EXCEPT

   (a) reducing employee empowerment.
   (b) reducing waste.
   (c) improving quality.
   (d) decreasing cycle time.

Completion

1. The role of management accounting information is shifting from a ____Command____-and-____Control____ philosophy to an ____inform____-and-____Improve____ philosophy.

2. The design and introduction of new measurements and systems must anticipate ____behavior____ and ____organizational____ reactions to the measurements.

3. In contrast to traditional costing systems that emphasize analysis within departmental and functional boundaries, an activity-based approach facilitates a ____Cross____-____Functional____ approach.

4. Studying how other best-performing organizations, either internal or external to the firm, perform similar activities or processes, is called benchmarking.

5. Management accounting serves several functions: operational, product costing ______, customer costing, management control, and strategic control.

6. Decentralized Responsibility refers to the authority that local division managers have to make decisions on pricing and product mix based on their superior access to local information.

7. Allowing employees to take initiative without explicit authorization from middle managers and executives has come to be known as employee empowerment.

8. The measurement of activities, which can be viewed as the mechanism by which organizational resources and employees accomplish work, will be the key organizing principle for studying management accounting information.

9. Flexible budgets provide forecasts of what expenses should have been, given the actual volume and mix of production and sales in the most recent period.

10. The Balanced Scorecard includes financial measures of performance, but adds the following measures from three additional perspectives: Customer, Internal Business Processes, and learning and growth.

Problems

1. Assume that you are designing a management accounting system for an express mail delivery service. Determine the management accounting information needs for each of the following employees:

   (a) delivery people.
   (b) local manager.
   (c) regional manager.

2. Contrast manufacturing and service organizations and how their management accounting information needs might differ.

SOLUTIONS TO PRACTICE TEST QUESTIONS AND PROBLEMS

True/False

1. True. Management accounting information encompasses all of these functions as it produces information that helps workers, managers, and executives make better decisions and improve processes and performance..

2. False. Management accounting information is generated for use primarily by constituencies internal to the firm.

3. False. Management accounting is not regulated by the government. Recall that management accounting information is generated primarily for use by individuals within an organization.

4. True. Management accounting information encompasses not only operational and nonfinancial information, such as quality and process times, but also measures of customer satisfaction and new product performance.

5. True. Managers should design systems that provide information useful for an organization's managers and employees.

6. True. During the last quarter of the twentieth century, both manufacturing and service organizations have discovered a need for improved management accounting information as they face increasingly challenging competitive environments.

7. False. Activities are the central focus on the organization.

8. False. A flexible budget is one that provides a forecast of what expenses should have been, given the actual volume and mix of production and sales in the most recent period.

9. True. Activity-based costing systems avoid arbitrary cost allocations that lead to subsequent cost distortions.

10. True. Demands for management accounting information will differ depending on the level of the organization, such as the operator level, the middle management level, and the top executive level.

Multiple-Choice

1. a. Management accounting information is not developed for shareholders.

2. c. Management accounting information is used for management control.

3. d. Critical success factors pertain to the long-term profitability of the firm.

4. b. ROI is equal to Operating Income/Investment. Therefore, ROI = $15,000/$300,000 = 5%. ROI can also be written as (Operating Income/Sales) × (Sales/Investment) = ($15,000/$120,000) × ($120,000/$300,000) = (12.5%)(40%) = 5%.

5. a. The Balanced Scorecard translates an organization's mission and strategy into performance measures from four perspectives: financial, customer, internal business processes, and learning and growth. A focus on the broad scope of business processes facilitates improvement in each of the four evaluation areas.

6. c. Customer costing is useful for determining the cost of serving each customer. Customer costing can include assignments of marketing, selling, distribution, and administrative costs to individual customers.

7. d. Flexible budgets take volume and mix of production and sales into account in providing an estimate of what expenses should have been for that volume and mix.

8. b Historically, service companies have used management accounting information less intensively than manufacturing companies.

9. c. The first step in using activity-based costing is to assign resource costs to activities.

10. a. Reducing employee empowerment is not a goal of continuous improvement. Rather, employee empowerment to correct problems as detected is an excellent means of encouraging continuous improvement.

Completion

1. command, control, inform, improve

2. behavioral, organizational

3. cross functional

4. benchmarking

5. product costing, customer costing, strategic control

6. Decentralized responsibility

7. employee empowerment

8. activities

9. Flexible budgets

10. customer, internal business processes, learning and growth

Problems

1. While no one correct response to this question exists, some possible answers follow.

   (a) Delivery people will probably want to know what the standards of work performance are on several dimensions so that they have a gauge on what is expected at work. They also need feedback information about their average delivery time per package, resources used (such as fuel), amount of breakage of package contents, etc.

   (b) The local manager will want summary information about each delivery person on such dimensions as on-time delivery, number of errors, breakage, resources spent per driver, customer satisfaction, number of speeding/parking tickets, and number of deliveries made. These measures will probably be recorded on a daily or weekly basis and compared to work standards that have been established.

(c) The regional manager will want to see weekly or monthly summaries of all of the delivery stations in his or her area. The summaries will include the average cost per delivery, volume of packages delivered, amount of breakage, number of customer complaints, and overall profitability of delivery stations.

2. While manufacturing companies produce products, service companies generally do not produce anything that can be inventoried. Service firms rely a great deal on human interaction. For instance, dealing with a bank teller or buying insurance from an insurance agent are examples where human interaction is important. On the other hand, when one buys an automobile, one owns a tangible product that can be evaluated by how the car handles, what it looks like, the quality of the components, etc. Quality can be assessed and controlled for products in a much easier way than for services. Often a defect can be corrected on an assembly line, but an uncomfortable ride or a rude flight attendant can be difficult or impossible to control in advance. Thus, services are subject to much more direct customer satisfaction and dissatisfaction than is manufacturing.

Notes and Questions

Chapter 2

The Organization as a System of Activities

CENTRAL FOCUS AND LEARNING OBJECTIVES

After reading this chapter you will be able to

1. understand the idea of the organization as a sequence of activities in a value chain.
2. appreciate the role of the customer in defining the focus of the activities in the value chain.
3. discuss the nature of value-added and nonvalue-added activities.
4. understand the role of performance measures in helping organization members manage the value chain.

REVIEW OF KEY TERMS AND CONCEPTS

Learning Objective 1:	Understand the idea of the organization as a sequence of activities in a value chain.

I. The Organization as a Sequence of Activities or Value Chain

A. Organizations perform a sequence of *activities* that provide goods or services, called *products*, to their *customers*.

B. A **value chain** is a sequence of activities whose objective is to provide a product to a customer or to provide an intermediate good or service in a larger value chain. *Each step in the value chain should add something that the **customer values** in the product or service.*

C. An **activity** is a unit of work, or task, with a specific goal. Examples of activities are processing an insurance claim, waiting on a customer in a restaurant, and welding two components together. There are four broad categories of activities in the value chain (see Exhibit 2-1):

1. **Input activities:** those relating to getting ready to make a product or provide a service.

2. **Processing activities:** those related to producing the product or service.

3. **Output activities:** those related to dealing with a customer.

4. **Administrative activities:** those that support 1 to 3 above, including human resources and general administration.

Learning Objective 2:	Appreciate the role of the customer in defining the focus of the activities in the value chain.

D. The Customer's Perspective: Each link in the entire value chain is the customer of the previous link (see Exhibit 2-2). For example, employees in one department should think of the employees in the next processing department as their customers, and focus on meeting those customers' needs.

E. Tempering the Customer Focus: The focus on customers may be modified because of the organization's objectives, as defined by the organization's owners, or because of the interests of the other stakeholders. **Stakeholders** are groups of people who have a legitimate claim on having an organization's objectives reflect their requirements. Each contributes to the organization and wants something in return. Stakeholders include:

1. Employees
2. Partners
3. Owners
4. The community
5. Customers

II. The Organization's Purpose

A. An organization's **objectives** are its broad purposes that reflect the objectives of the stakeholders whose interests the organization deems primary.

B. **Organization control** is the activity of assessing the value chain's performance from the perspective of the organization's objectives. Note that an effective planning and control system should factor in the objectives and strategies of the organization.

C. **Process control** is the activity of assessing the operating performance of a single process of the entire value chain in meeting customer requirements. Process control compares short-term performance to short-run targets or standards, and focuses on directing, evaluating, and improving the processes the organization uses to deliver products to its customers.

Carefully study Exhibit 2-3, which shows the interrelationships among stakeholders, the value chain, and organizational objectives. Do you see similarity between this exhibit and the Balanced Scorecard approach in Chapter 1?

Learning Objective 3: Discuss the nature of value-added and nonvalue-added activities.

Learning Objective 4: Understand the role of performance measures in helping organization members manage the value chain.

III. Performance Measures in Process Control

A. **Critical success factors** are elements of performance required for an organization's success. Three of these are related to the ability of the organization to meet customer requirements:

1. **Service** consists of the product's tangible and intangible features promised to the customer; service is also known as value in use.

2. **Quality** is the difference between the promised and the realized level of service. Quality is also defined as conformance to specifications.

3. **Costs** reflect the resources used to provide products or services.

B. **Critical performance indicators** are performance measures used to assess an organization's performance on its critical success factors.

Review Exhibits 2-4 and 2-5, which illustrate elements of and the relationship between service and quality. Review Exhibit 2-6 to see the linkage between critical success factors and critical performance indicators. Be sure that you understand the relationship between the two.

C. The Nature of Effective and Efficient

1. A process is **effective** if it meets its objectives.

2. A process is **efficient** if it achieves its objectives using the fewest possible resources.

IV. **Performance measurement** is the activity of measuring the performance of an activity or a value chain.

A. An effective system of operations performance measurement includes critical performance indicators that:

1. consider each activity from the **customer's perspective.**

2. evaluate each activity using **customer-validated measures of performance.**

   a. An **output** is a physical measure of production or activity, such as the number of units produced or the amount of time spent doing something.

   b. An **outcome** is the *value* the customer attributes to the result of an activity, such as the number of good units of production and the amount of client satisfaction generated by a service.

   c. The critical difference between outcome and output measurement is that outcome focuses on effectiveness in meeting customer requirements, and output does not (see Exhibits 2-7 and 2-8).

3. are **comprehensive** in considering all facets of activity performance for customers.

4. provide **feedback** to organizational employees on how to identify problems and improve.

V. Signals

A. A **signal** is information provided to a decision-maker. There are two types of signals:

1. A **warning** that there is a problem.

2. A **diagnostic** that identifies the problem.

B. **Costs and benefits of signals**: Companies should evaluate all management accounting information and control systems, at least intuitively, by comparing the costs and benefits of the proposed information and system.

VI. Performance Standards

A. **Control** is the set of methods and tools that organization members use to keep the organization on track toward achieving its objectives. Control may be exercised by:

1. developing standard procedures and ensuring compliance with the procedures. Information is used to motivate people to follow procedures and to verify that they follow them.

2. hiring qualified people who understand the organization's objectives and giving them authority to make decisions to help the organization achieve its objectives. Information is provided to these people to facilitate their decision-making.

B. **Managing by the numbers** is an approach to cost-cutting that focuses on reducing the budget, or cost allowance, allowed for a particular activity. Managing by the numbers has the following three problems:

1. It is ineffective.

2. It assumes that cost is the only relevant measure of an activity's performance.

3. It does not recognize the reasons that costs exist.

C. A more effective method of cost control involves understanding how customer requirements create the need for activities, how activities create costs, and what activities add value. See Exhibit 2-10 and the definition of *activity-based management* in Chapter 1.

1. A **value-added activity** is one that, if eliminated, would reduce the product's service to the customer.

2. A **nonvalue-added activity** is an activity that presents the opportunity for cost reduction without reducing the product's service potential to the customer.

3. Continuous improvement treats the existing process as given and tries to make it less costly. Specifically, **continuous improvement** is the relentless search to:

   a. document, understand, and improve the activities that the organization undertakes to meet its customers' requirements.

   b. eliminate nonvalue-added activities.

   c. improve the performance of value-added activities.

4. **Re-engineering** involves evaluating the process objectives and redesigning the entire process to make it less costly. Re-engineering can also involve finding and eliminating nonvalue-added activities.

D. **Activity analysis (value analysis)** is an approach to operations control that involves applying the steps of continuous improvement to an activity. Four steps are involved:

   1. **Identify** the process objectives.

   2. **Chart** by **recording** from start to finish the activities used to complete a product or service. **Storyboarding** is an example of charting.

   3. **Classify** all activities as value-added or nonvalue-added.

   4. **Continuously improve** the efficiency of all activities and plan to eliminate nonvalue-added activities.

Be sure you understand the fundamental concepts of this chapter. The perspective that the organization is a sequence of activities in a value chain forms the foundation for the remainder of this book. Management accounting, described as "information that creates value" in Chapter 1, helps organization members manage the value chain.

PRACTICE TEST QUESTIONS AND PROBLEMS

True/False

____ 1. Stakeholders to the organization include employees, partners, and the community.

____ 2. Each step in a value chain should add something that the customer values to a product.

____ 3. *Effectiveness* means using the fewest possible resources to meet stated objectives.

____ 4. Quality is usually defined in the abstract, independent of a service or product.

____ 5. Outputs and outcomes are identical.

____ 6. Performance measures involve two types of signals: warning and diagnostic.

____ 7. Because accurate information is so critical in today's competitive environment, organizations should pursue improved information systems no matter what the cost.

____ 8. One of the problems in "managing by the numbers" is that it simply takes too long.

____ 9. The design of an effective management accounting system should be contingent on the unique nature of the organization, its objectives, and its strategies.

____ 10. Output measurement does not focus on effectiveness in meeting customer requirements.

Multiple-Choice

1. Each of the following is an input activity in the value chain, EXCEPT

   (a) research and development.
   (b) hiring and training employees.
   (c) buying raw materials.
   (d) moving work-in-process.

2. An organization is efficient if

   (a) it achieves its objectives.
   (b) it uses the fewest resources possible to achieve its objectives.
   (c) it uses the largest amount of resources possible to achieve its objectives.
   (d) total planned output is achieved regardless of inputs used.

3. Choose the best answer to finish the sentence, "When quality goes up, ..."

   (a) scrap goes up.
   (b) rework goes up.
   (c) costs go down.
   (d) costs go up.

4. A value-added activity, if eliminated, would

   (a) reduce the product's service to the customer.
   (b) increase the product's service to the customer.
   (c) have no effect on the product's service to the customer.
   (d) increase the cost of the product.

5. An effective performance measurement system contains critical performance indicators that do each of the following, EXCEPT

   (a) consider each activity and the organization itself from the customer's perspective.
   (b) evaluate each activity using customer-validated measures.
   (c) provide feedback to help identify problems.
   (d) consider each activity and the organization itself only from an internal management perspective.

6. Control is

   (a) the relentless search to find ways to improve the organization.
   (b) applicable only in manufacturing organizations.
   (c) the set of methods and tools that organization members use to keep the organization on track toward achieving its objectives.
   (d) an organization's search for the best way to do something as practiced by another organization.

7. Continuous improvement involves all of the following EXCEPT

   (a) understanding the activities that the organization undertakes to meet its customers' requirements.
   (b) improving the performance of value-added activities.
   (c) redesigning entire processes.
   (d) eliminating nonvalue-added activities.

8. Process control involves all of the following EXCEPT

   (a) comparing short-term performance to appropriate standards.
   (b) evaluating the organization's processes.
   (c) improving the organization's processes.
   (d) assessing a value chain's performance from the organization's perspective.

9. Which of the following is NOT one of the four broad classes of activities in the value chain?

   (a) Re-engineering activities
   (b) Processing activities
   (c) Output activities
   (d) Administrative activities

10. The domain of management accounting includes all of the following EXCEPT

   (a) comparison of the organization's actual performance with objectives.
   (b) assessment of customer satisfaction with products.
   (c) evaluation of processes within the organization.
   (d) preparation of statements required for external reporting.

Completion

1. Most organizations have five groups of stakeholders: the employees, ____________, ____________, ____________, and ____________.

2. An activity is a unit of ____________ with a specific ____________.

3. Organizations perform a sequence of ____________ that provide goods or services to their customers.

4. A ____________ ____________ is a sequence of activities whose objective is to provide a product to a customer or to provide an intermediate good or service in a larger ____________ ____________.

5. Three critical success factors related to the ability of an organization to meet customer requirements are ____________, ____________, and ____________.

6. Service refers to the product's ____________ ____________, such as performance and taste, and its ____________ ____________, such as how people are treated when making the purchase decision.

7. Quality is the difference between the ____________ and ____________ level of service.

8. An ____________ is how the customer values the result of an activity.

9. A ____________ signal suggests what the problem is.

10. Phil Crosby, one of the 1980s' noted quality gurus, argued that "“Quality is ____________.”

Problems

1. What are the critical success factors for a major airline?

2. List as many nonvalue-added activities involved in a manufacturing facility as you can. Can all of these be eliminated, and, if so, how?

SOLUTIONS TO PRACTICE TEST QUESTIONS AND PROBLEMS

True/False

1. True. All are organizational stakeholders.

2. True. Each step in the value chain should add value to the customer.

3. False. This is the definition of efficiency.

4. False. Quality is defined relative to the product or service.

5. False. Outputs are a physical measure of activity, while outcomes are the values attributed to the output by the customer.

6. True. These are the two types of signals.

7. False. The costs and benefits of the improved information should be assessed, at least intuitively.

8. False. There are three problems, but length of time is not one of them.

9. True. A management accounting system must take into account the organizational context in which it is used.

10. True. An output is a physical measure of production or activity. *Outcome* focuses on effectiveness in meeting customer requirements.

Multiple-Choice

1. d. Moving work-in-process is not an input activity in the value chain; rather, it is a processing activity.

2. b. An organization is efficient if it uses the fewest resources possible to achieve its objectives.

3. c. When quality goes up, costs often go down, because of reduced scrap, fewer defects, and lower warranty costs.

4. a. By the definition of value-added, the product's service to the customer would go down.

5. d. The key is the customer's perspective, not internal management's.

6. c. Control consists of a set of tools and methods to keep the organization on track.

7. c. Continuous improvement treats existing processes as given and tries to make them less costly; response d describes re-engineering, which involves evaluating process objectives and redesigning entire processes.

8. d. Process control involves all of the responses except d, which refers to organization control.

9. a. The fourth class of activities consists of input activities.

10. d. Preparation of statements required for external reporting is in the domain of financial accounting.

Completion

1. partners, owners, community, customers
2. work, goal
3. activities
4. value chain
5. service, quality, costs
6. tangible features, intangible features
7. promised, realized
8. outcome
9. diagnostic
10. free

Problems

1. The critical success factors for a major airline are:

   (a) providing safe planes. Planes must be maintained and inspected carefully on a regular basis and no defects tolerated.

   (b) price of tickets. Ticket prices are critical given the level of competition.

   (c) on-time departure and arrival. This means that the ticket collection and seating procedures must be efficient, and the plane must be fueled, serviced, and inspected, and baggage loaded promptly.

   (d) passenger comfort and service. Seating should be comfortable, meals good (or at least edible!), flight attendants courteous, and flight attendants must also be able to deal with difficult passengers and other problems that arise.

   Excellent performance on all of these factors will lead to the most critical variable of all, which is **repeat business.**

2. The broad categories of nonvalue-added activities typically include moving raw materials and work-in-process, storing these items, and inspecting them. Each of these three activities doesn't really add anything to the product that the customer values. However, each activity may be necessary, depending on the way the production facility is designed. One way to eliminate all of these activities is to employ a manufacturing philosophy such as just-in-time (JIT). Under this philosophy, raw materials are delivered by outside vendors, just as they are needed. Work-in-process is eliminated because the JIT system allows only one unit to be worked on at a time. Further, under JIT, since each employee is responsible for quality, there is no need for a separate inspection department of personnel. If it is not possible to use a full-blown JIT system, some aspects of the philosophy can be employed.

Notes and Questions

Chapter 3

Cost Concepts

CENTRAL FOCUS AND LEARNING OBJECTIVES

After reading this chapter, you will be able to

1. classify costs based on their functions.
2. differentiate between direct and indirect costs.
3. understand how support activity costs arise.
4. discuss unit-related, batch-related, product-sustaining, and facility-sustaining activity cost drivers.
5. express the cost relations of activities and their drivers as equations.
6. discuss how to collect information to estimate activity costs.
7. extend cost concepts to service organizations.
8. determine standard costs.
9. understand the uses and limitations of standard cost systems.

REVIEW OF KEY TERMS AND CONCEPTS

Learning Objective 1: Classify costs based on their functions.

I. Functional Cost Classifications in Traditional Systems

A. Costs versus Expenses

1. **Cost** is the monetary value of goods and services expended to obtain current or future benefits.

2. **Expenses** are either costs for which benefits were already derived in the current period (such as cost of goods sold), or costs whose benefits cannot be matched easily with the products or services of another period (such as advertising).

B. Product versus Period Costs

1. **Product costs** are costs associated with the manufacture of products.

2. **Period costs** are costs treated as expenses in the period in which they are incurred because they cannot be associated with the manufacture of products.

3. **Production volume** is the overall measure, such as number of units, of various products manufactured in a given time period.

C. Manufacturing versus Nonmanufacturing Costs

1. **Manufacturing costs** are all costs of transforming raw materials into finished product. Traditionally only manufacturing costs are included when valuing finished goods inventory and only manufacturing costs are considered product costs.

2. **Nonmanufacturing costs** are all costs other than manufacturing costs. Traditionally, these costs are considered period costs and are expenses in the period in which they are incurred. These include:

a. **Distribution costs**, which include costs of delivering finished products to customers.

b. **Selling costs**, which include sales personnel salaries and commissions and other sales office expenses.

c. **Marketing costs**, which include advertising and publicity expenses.

d. **Research and development costs**, which include expenditures for designing and bringing new products to market.

e. **General and administrative costs** which include expenses such as the CEO's salary, legal and general accounting costs, and those costs that do not come under any of the other categories listed.

Learning Objective 2: Differentiate between direct and indirect costs.

D. Direct versus Indirect Costs

1. **Direct costs** are those that can be traced easily to the product manufactured or service rendered. Direct manufacturing costs are assigned to products directly, based on the measured quantity of *resources consumed* for their manufacture. Examples are:

a. **Direct materials cost**—the cost of all materials and parts that can be traced directly to the product.

b. **Direct labor cost**—wages and fringe benefits paid to workers involved directly in manufacturing a product.

Review equation (3-1):

$$C = P \times Q$$

C = cost of input resource
P = price per unit of resource
Q = quantity of resource

Learning Objective 3: Understand how support activity costs arise.

2. **Indirect costs** are those that cannot be traced easily to products or services produced; also referred to as support costs. **Manufacturing support costs** (or overhead or burden) are indirect costs of transforming raw materials into finished product; indirect manufacturing costs. Examples include:

   a. Wages and benefits paid to **production supervisors** who do not directly produce the product.

   b. Wages and benefits paid to **other support personnel** who are involved with scheduling, moving materials, inspection, etc.

Do you understand all of these terms? Note the contrasting pairs of pairs of concepts, especially between the functions of manufacturing versus nonmanufacturing, and how they relate to determination of product costs for inventory valuation and cost of goods sold for external financial reporting.

II. Recent Changes in Manufacturing Cost Structure

A. The proportion of direct labor in the early 1900s could have been as high as 50% of unit product cost. Today direct labor cost may be as small as 5% of unit product cost.

B. The proportion of support (overhead) costs has increased because of the shift toward greater automation, the emphasis on better customer service, and the proliferation of multiple products. Therefore, designers of new cost systems are now paying much more attention to **support costs** and the activities that generate them.

Learning Objective 4: Discuss unit-related, batch-related, product-sustaining, and facility-sustaining activity cost drivers.

III. Activity-Based Analysis of Indirect and Support Costs

A. Types of Production Activities

1. **Unit-related activities** are those whose levels are related to the number of units produced. Example: energy required to operate manufacturing machinery.

2. **Batch-related activities** are those whose levels are related to the number of batches produced. Example: machine setups.

3. **Product-sustaining activities** are those activities performed to support the production and sale of individual products. Example: improving ice cream flavor recipes.

4. **Facility-sustaining activities** are those performed to provide the managerial infrastructure and to support the upkeep of the plant. Example: plant management.

This classification scheme of activities is extremely important; we will return to it frequently.

Learning Objective 5: Express the cost relations of activities and their drivers as equations.

Learning Objective 6: Discuss how to collect information to estimate activity costs.

B. Activity Cost Drivers

1. **Activity cost driver** is a unit of measurement for the level (or quantity) of the activity performed (see examples in Exhibit 3-3).

2. **Activity cost driver rate** is the ratio of the cost of resources to provide an activity to the level of the capacity made available by those resources. Note that the cost of activities depends on the available **capacity** of the driver rather than the actual use of the capacity (see the example below equation (3-3)).

Review equation (3-2):

$C = R \times X$

where

C = activity cost
R = the cost driver rate for the activity
X = the surrogate cost driver measure for the activity

R is determined from equation (3-3): $R = C \div X$

Review equations (3-4), (3-5), and (3-6) on multiple activities and cost distortion.

Equation (3-5) for multiple activities:

$$C = C_1 + C_2 + C_3 + C_4 + C_5$$

$$= R_1 \times X_1 + R_2 \times X_2 + R_3 \times X_3 + R_4 \times X_4 + R_5 \times X_5$$

Carefully work through the review problem on Goodhue Steel Tubes, Inc., and the Montex Company Illustration.

Learning Objective 7: Extend cost concepts to service organizations.

IV. Cost Concepts for Service Organizations

A. Services produced cannot be inventoried for future sale. Thus, cost accounting systems associated with most service organizations do not have to worry about financial reporting requirements of inventory valuation.

B. Regulatory requirements for financial reporting for services often specify the structure of cost reports.

C. Output is difficult to measure as services produce less tangible and measurable products than manufacturing organizations.

D. Indirect costs of producing services in a service organization are often referred to as **operating costs**.

Learning Objective 8: Determine standard costs.

Learning Objective 9: Understand the uses and limitations of standard cost systems.

V. Standard Cost Accounting Systems

A. **Standard costs** are efficient and attainable benchmarks established in advance for the costs of activity resources that should be consumed by each product. Standard cost systems are used for three main reasons:

1. Estimate product costs.

2. Budget for costs and expenditures.

3. Control costs relative to standards. **Cost variances** arise when there are differences between standards and actual costs.

B. Standards should be set at levels that are efficient and attainable.

C. Standard costing systems are most useful when production technology is stable.

PRACTICE TEST QUESTIONS AND PROBLEMS

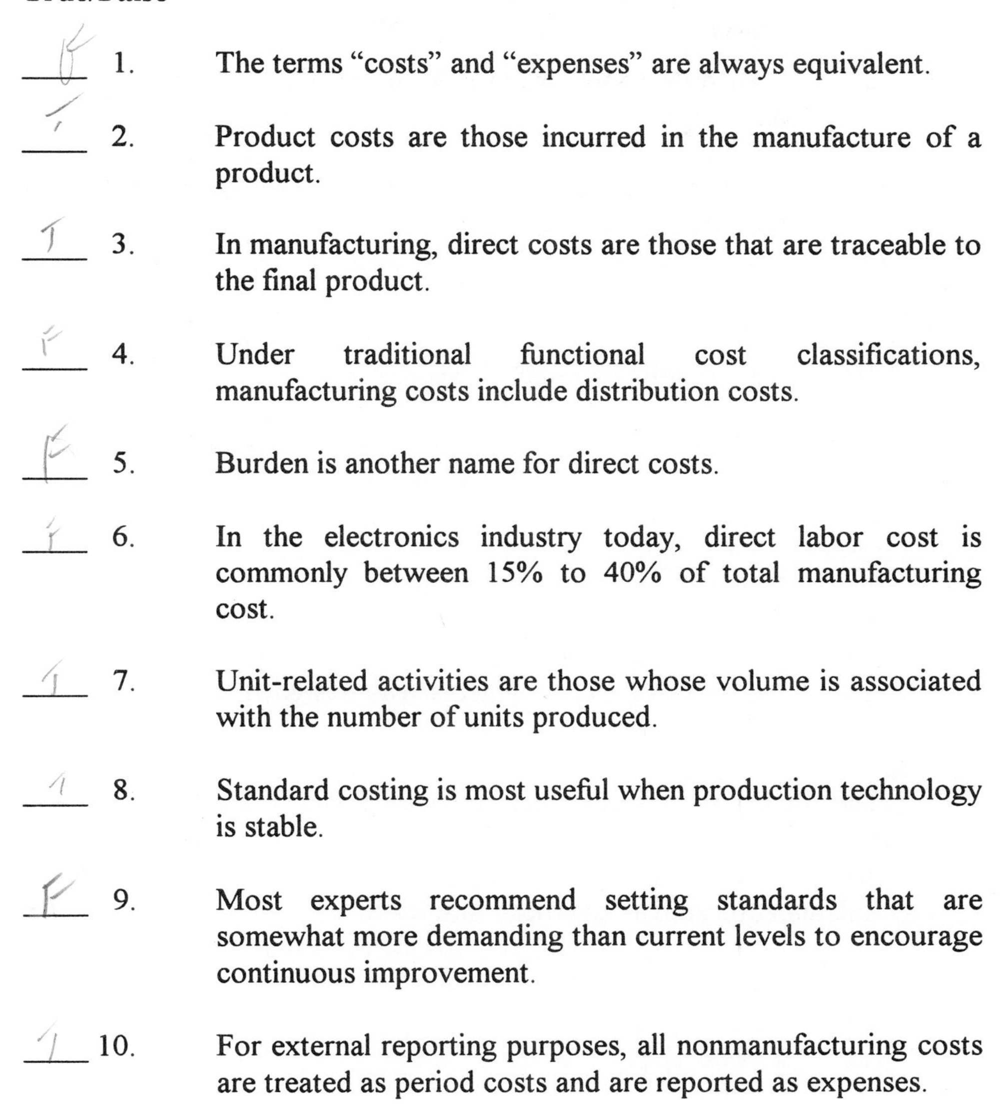

True/False

____ 1. The terms “costs” and “expenses” are always equivalent.

____ 2. Product costs are those incurred in the manufacture of a product.

____ 3. In manufacturing, direct costs are those that are traceable to the final product.

____ 4. Under traditional functional cost classifications, manufacturing costs include distribution costs.

____ 5. Burden is another name for direct costs.

____ 6. In the electronics industry today, direct labor cost is commonly between 15% to 40% of total manufacturing cost.

____ 7. Unit-related activities are those whose volume is associated with the number of units produced.

____ 8. Standard costing is most useful when production technology is stable.

____ 9. Most experts recommend setting standards that are somewhat more demanding than current levels to encourage continuous improvement.

____ 10. For external reporting purposes, all nonmanufacturing costs are treated as period costs and are reported as expenses.

Multiple-Choice

1. Period costs include those

    (a) incurred for the manufacture of a product.
    (b) whose benefits cannot be matched easily with the products of a specific period.
    (c) that are directly traceable to a product.
    (d) incurred to pay direct labor workers.

2. Product costs are those

(a) that are only indirectly traceable to a product.
(b) that include selling costs of the good produced.
(c) that include only manufacturing overhead.
(d) incurred for the manufacture of a product.

3. Nonmanufacturing costs include each of the following, EXCEPT

(a) direct materials costs.
(b) distribution costs.
(c) marketing costs.
(d) general administrative costs.

4. In a car manufacturing firm using a traditional cost accounting system for external reporting, manufacturing costs include each of the following, EXCEPT

(a) the cost of steel for each automobile chassis.
(b) the cost of tires for each car.
(c) the cost of janitorial services in the factory.
(d) the cost of design engineers who designed the cars that are manufactured.

5. The total cost of performing activities S and Y are $130,000 and $100,000, respectively, and the total number of units of the cost driver for activity S and Y are 10,000 and 25,000, respectively. Calculate the activity overhead rate for S.

(a) $ 8.52
(b) $ 9.20
(c) $ 4.00
(d) $13.00

6. If a true cost equation has two cost drivers, but only one driver is used, what problem can arise?

(a) No problems whatsoever.
(b) Costs will actually be more accurate.
(c) Cost distortion can occur.
(d) Cost accounting becomes more complex.

7. The cost equation for manufacturing support costs for Bonnes Company has two activity drivers, DLH, direct labor hours and MH, machine hours. The cost equation is given by C = $25 × DLH + $120 × MH. The values for the activity cost drivers for March are 700 direct labor hours and 40 machine hours. Calculate C, the estimated total manufacturing support costs for the Bonnes Company, for March.

   (a) $22,300
   (b) $85,000
   (c) $17,500
   (d) $ 4,800

8. Product-sustaining activities include all of the following, EXCEPT

   (a) maintenance of drawings and machine routings for parts.
   (b) engineering efforts to perform product enhancements.
   (c) obtaining patents.
   (d) machine setups. BATCH related

9. Indirect costs in service organizations are often referred to as

   (a) service expenses.
   (b) standard expenses.
   (c) operating costs.
   (d) operating standards.

10. Which of the following is NOT a major reason for using standard cost systems?

   (a) Budgeting for costs and expenditures
   (b) Controlling costs relative to standards
   (c) Eliminating the need for activity-based costing
   (d) Estimating product costs

Completion

1. Most cost accounting systems calculate product costs for product pricing and product __mix__ decisions.

2. Cost is defined as the monetary value of goods and services expended to obtain current or __future__ benefits.

3. Manufacturing costs include all costs of ______________ raw materials into finished product.

4. One notable change in manufacturing cost structure today is that the share of ______________ ______________ costs has become increasingly important.

5. Production activities are classified into the following four categories: __________ - ______________, __________ - ______________, ______________ - ______________, and ______________ ______________ activities.

6. The activity cost driver rate is the ratio of the cost of resources to provide an activity to the level of the ______________ made available by those resources.

7. Unlike in manufacturing organizations, the __________ __________ of a service organization can be difficult to measure.

8. The portion of product costs assigned to the products and sold in a period appears as __________ ______ __________ __________ expense on the income statement; the remaining portion of the product costs appears as an __________ on the __________ __________.

9. The differences between ______________ and ______________ costs are called cost variances.

10. A standard set at an average level that is easy to achieve will not ______________ workers to exert more effort to eliminate existing inefficiencies.

Problems

1. The manufacturing support costs of the machining plant of Diamond Company are represented by the following equation:

$$\text{SUPPCOST} = \$135 \times \text{SETUP} + \$9.80 \times \text{DLH} + \$5.5 \times \text{MHCAP}$$

where

SUPPCOST	=	manufacturing support cost
SETUP	=	the number of setups
DLH	=	direct labor hours
MHCAP	=	the machine-hour capacity available

The planned levels of the cost drivers for January and February are:

	SETUP	DLH	MHCAP
January	50	700	990
February	120	670	2000

What is the expected level of manufacturing support costs for January and for February?

2. Rosso Company estimated its manufacturing support costs (MFGSUPP) as 88% of its direct labor cost (DLCOST):
MFGSUPP $= 0.88 \times$ DLCOST

Syd Young decided to analyze the activities at the plant in detail and found that support costs were incurred to perform activities related to machine setup (SETUPS), inspecting finished products (INSPECT), and shipping products (SHPMNTS). He developed the following equation to estimate manufacturing support costs:

MFGSUPP $=$ \$0.70 $\times$ DLCOST $+$ \$40 $\times$ SETUPS $+$ \$ 23 $\times$ INSPECT $+$ \$34 $\times$ SHPMNTS

Planned activities for July and August are as follows:

	DLCOST	SETUPS	INSPECT	SHPMNTS
July	15,000	20	15	30
August	21,500	26	18	35

(a) Estimate the expected amount of manufacturing support costs for July and for August using the old equation based only on direct labor cost.

(b) Estimate the expected amount of manufacturing support costs for July and for August using the new equation developed by Syd Young.

(c) Why is there a difference between the two sets of estimates? Which set of estimates is likely to be more accurate? Why?

SOLUTIONS TO PRACTICE TEST QUESTIONS AND PROBLEMS

True/False

1. False. Costs and expenses can be the same, but not in every situation. For example, costs associated with goods produced but not sold appear as an asset on the balance sheet; the costs appear as expenses on the income statement when the goods are sold.

2. True. This is the definition of product costs.

3. True. In manufacturing product costing, this is the definition of direct costs.

4. False. Distribution costs are marketing costs and come under the general heading of nonmanufacturing costs.

5. False. Burden is another name for overhead.

6. False. Direct labor cost is often less than 5% of total manufacturing cost.

7. True. This is the definition of unit-related activities.

8. True. In contrast, when the organization's competitive environment requires constant innovation that anticipates customer needs, overreliance on past standards can be detrimental to the organization's progress.

9. False. Most experts recommend setting standards that are *efficient* and *attainable* operating procedures.

10. True. For external reporting purposes, nonmanufacturing costs are treated as period costs and are reported as expenses, usually without the detailed analysis performed on manufacturing costs.

Multiple-Choice

1. b. This is the definition of period costs.

2. d This is the definition of product costs.

3. a. Direct materials cost is a manufacturing cost.

4. d. Responses a and b are classified as direct materials, and response c is classified as a manufacturing support costs. For external reporting, response d is classified as a nonmanufacturing (period) cost.

5. d. The overhead rate for activity S = $130,000/10,000 = $13.00.

6. c. Cost distortion will occur, as both activity drivers are not recognized.

7. a. C = $25 (700) + $120(40) = $22,300.

8. d Machine setups are considered a batch-related activity.

9. c. *Operating costs* is the correct answer.

10. c. Standard costs do not eliminate the need for activity-based costing. The example of Jim and Barry's ice cream operation demonstrates the effective use of standard costs with activity-based costing.

Completion

1. mix
2. future
3. transforming
4. manufacturing support
5. Unit related, batch related, product sustaining, facility sustaining
6. capacity
7. true output
8. cost of goods sold, asset, balance sheet
9. actual, standard
10. motivate

Problems

1. January: \$19,055 ($\$135 \times 50 + \$9.8 \times 700 + \$5.5 \times 990$)

   February: \$33,766 ($\$135 \times 120 + \$9.8 \times 670 + \$5.5 \times 2000$)

2. (a) Estimated manufacturing support costs based on direct labor cost:

   July: $0.88 \times \$15{,}000 = \$13{,}200$
   August: $0.88 \times \$21{,}500 = \$18{,}920$

   (b) Estimated manufacturing support costs based on the new equation:

   July: $\$0.7 \times 15{,}000 + \$40 \times 20 + \$23 \times 15 + \$34 \times 30$
   $= \$12{,}665$
   August: $\$0.7 \times 21{,}500 + \$40 \times 26 + \$23 \times 18 + \$34 \times 35$
   $= \$17{,}694$

   (c) The two sets of estimates differ because important cost drivers were left out in the old equation. The estimates based on the new equation are more accurate, as the new cost drivers are included. Note that the sum of the costs for the two months under the old equation is not equivalent to the sum under the new equation.

Notes and Questions

Chapter 4

Cost Behavior

CENTRAL FOCUS AND LEARNING OBJECTIVES

After reading this chapter, you will be able to

1. identify the difference between fixed and variable costs.
2. understand the significance of breakeven analysis in decision-making.
3. capture the relationship among revenues, costs incurred, and production volumes by sketching a planning model.
4. discuss the importance of knowing how the commitment and usage of activity resources influence cost variability.
5. understand the significance of the normal costs of an activity.
6. explain why activity costs tend to be variable in the long run.
7. link the costs of support resources to the production of multiple products.
8. understand the difference between the costs of resources supplied and the costs of resources used for an activity.

REVIEW OF KEY TERMS AND CONCEPTS

Learning Objective 1: Identify the difference between fixed and variable costs.

I. Cost Behavior and Production Volume

Managers are concerned with how costs change with changes in the level of one key cost driver: the volume of production. Production (manufacturing) costs are classified as *fixed* or *variable*, as defined below, based on their relation to changes in production volume. *Nonmanufacturing costs (such as selling costs) are classified similarly.*

A. **Fixed costs** do not change with changes in the level of production over short periods of time. In other words, they are independent of the level of production.

B. **Variable costs** change in proportion to changes in production volume. They represent resources whose consumption can be adjusted to match the demand for them.

Study Exhibits 4-1 through 4-6 for examples. Do you understand the differences between fixed and variable costs?

C. **Mixed costs** are those composed of both fixed and variable cost components.

Study Exhibits 4-7 and 4-8 for examples.
Note Equation (4-1):

Total costs = Fixed costs + (Variable cost rate) × Quantity of production, or

$$C = F + (V \times Q)$$

D. Representing Activity Costs as Fixed or Variable

Many unit-related measures are closely related to production volume. However, over a sufficiently long period of time, when managers can adjust the level of resources for batch-related activities, some batch-related measures also may vary with production volume. See equations (4-2) and (4-3).

II. Costs in an Economic Framework

A. **A cost curve** is a graph of costs plotted against activity cost driver or production volume. See Exhibit 4-9.

B. **Economies of scale** means average costs decrease with increases in production volume.

C. **Capacity constraints** are limitations on the quantity that can be produced because the capacity committed for some activity resources (such as plant space, number of machines) cannot be changed in the short run.

D. **Diseconomies of scale** means average costs increase with increases in production volume.

E. **Relevant range** is the range of production levels over which the classification of a cost as fixed or variable is appropriate. Linear equations often provide good approximations of the behavior of costs within the relevant range.

III. The Step Function Cost Curve

When step cost functions apply, the linearity assumption of the cost equation does not hold.

See Exhibits 4-10 and 4-11 for illustrations.

A. **Step function cost curves** portray costs that increase in discrete steps.

B. **Step fixed costs** are those that increase in relatively wide discrete steps.

C. **Step variable costs** are those that increase in relatively narrow discrete steps.

Learning Objective 2: Understand the significance of breakeven analysis in decision-making.

IV. Breakeven Analysis

Breakeven analysis involves determining the level of production at which the profit resulting from one option is at least as large as the profit resulting from an alternative option.

A. **Breakeven point** is the point of intersection of the sales revenue curve and the total cost curve.

B. **Contribution margin per unit** is the difference between the sales price and variable cost per unit.

C. **Breakeven chart** is a set of graphs depicting the sales revenues and fixed, variable, and total costs.

D. The **contribution margin ratio** expresses the contribution margin as a percentage of sales.

Note in equation (4-6) that the *breakeven point* can be expressed as:

Breakeven point (in units) = Fixed costs/Contribution margin per unit

To determine how many units need to be sold to make a *target profit*, the breakeven point equation is modified to be:

Production volume = (Fixed costs + Target profit)/Contribution margin per unit.

If $1 is treated as the unit of measurement for the production level, the breakeven point formula is equivalent to:

Breakeven point (in sales dollars) =
Fixed costs/Contribution margin ratio

Learning Objective 3: Capture the relationship among revenues, costs incurred, and production volumes by sketching a planning model.

Exhibits 4-14, 4-15 and 4-16 outline how a planning model of cost and revenue behavior can be developed. Carefully work through the subsequent review problem.

Learning Objective 4: Discuss the importance of knowing how commitment and usage of activity resources influence cost variability.

V. Supply versus Usage of Activity Resources

A. The behavior of costs is contingent on time frame, range of activity levels, and other factors. Variable costs *represent resources whose consumption can be adjusted to match the demand placed on them.*

Study Exhibits 4-17 and 4-18.

Learning Objective 5: Understand the significance of the normal costs of an activity.

B. **Normal cost of an activity** is the average cost at the point where activity demand equals available capacity. It is the cost of providing the resource capacity made available for an activity.

In equation (4-9), *normal unit cost* is expressed as:

Normal unit cost = Regular cost of providing capacity/Capacity made available

Learning Objective 6: Explain why activity costs tend to be variable in the long run.

Learning Objective 7: Link the costs of support resources to the production of multiple products.

Learning Objective 8: Understand the difference between the costs of resources supplied and the costs of resources used for an activity.

VI. Resource Flexibility and Cost Variability

A. **Cost behavior** is a description of how costs change with changes in an activity cost driver or production volume. A key concept to understand regarding cost behavior is that for some production resources, managers must commit to providing resources, often before knowing what the actual demand for them will be. The cost of supplying resources will be incurred regardless of whether they will be fully used.

B. **Flexible resources** are those which are acquired as needed and whose costs vary with production activity.

C. **Discretionary costs** are those that result from strategic and tactical decisions of managers, such that the expenditure levels chosen influence the production volume instead of production volume influencing the consumption of activity resources.

D. **Committed resources** are those made available for an activity prior to knowing the demand for it. These resources cannot be reduced in case the demand turns out to be less than the capacity made available by the committed resources.

E. Activities may be associated with a direct or surrogate measure known as a **cost driver**. For example, the number of purchase orders is a driver for purchase department costs.

Exhibits 4-23 through 4-26 illustrate commitment and consumption of activity resources for multiple products. Exhibit 4-27 illustrates the contrast between resource supply and resource usage, and Exhibit 4-28 provides an example of computation of normal activity costs.

Carefully work through the summary example at the end of the chapter.

PRACTICE TEST QUESTIONS AND PROBLEMS

True/False

____ 1. Fixed costs change with changes in the level of production.

____ 2. Mixed costs are composed of two or more types of variable costs.

____ 3. Economies of scale means average costs decrease with increases in production volume.

____ 4. The relevant range holds for fixed costs only.

____ 5. A step variable cost is one that increases in relatively narrow discrete steps.

____ 6. The normal cost of an activity is the average cost at the point where activity demand equals available capacity.

____ 7. Expenditures for advertising and publicity are examples of discretionary costs.

____ 8. Committed resources are made available before their demand is known precisely.

____ 9. The contribution margin per unit is the difference between unit sales price and unit fixed cost.

____ 10. The breakeven point is the point of intersection of the sales revenue curve and the total cost curve.

Multiple-Choice

1. Variable costs per unit of product

   (a) change with changes in the level of production.
   (b) do not change with changes in the level of production.
   (c) are irrelevant in breakeven analysis.
   (d) are irrelevant in assessing selling costs.

2. Fixed cost per unit volume _________ when production increases.

(a) decreases
(b) increases slightly
(c) increases sharply
(d) stays the same

3. Neuf Company has just rented a copying machine for $110/month. Neuf also is being charged $0.04 for each copy made. It is estimated that Neuf will make 40,000 copies this month. What is Neuf's total cost of the copier for the month?

(a) $10,110
(b) $ 1,600
(c) $ 110
(d) $ 1,710

4. The relevant range in a step function cost curve is restricted to be

(a) over the entire step function cost curve.
(b) within several steps.
(c) within a step.
(d) within two steps.

5. Max Company has gathered the following information about its operations: The regular cost of providing capacity is $45,000, the total capacity is 500 jobs and the capacity made available is 375. What is the normal cost per job?

(a) $120 per job
(b) $ 90 per job
(c) $360 per job
(d) $125 per job

6. The use of discretionary resources is

(a) directly related to production volume.
(b) directly related to total support costs.
(c) directly related to total fixed costs.
(d) not directly related to the production volume.

7. Committed resources are made available before

   (a) their supply is known precisely.
   (b) their demand is known precisely.
   (c) both supply and demand are known precisely.
   (d) the end of each fiscal year.

8. Activities may be associated with a direct or surrogate measure referred to as a

   (a) discretionary cost.
   (b) step cost.
   (c) cost driver.
   (d) normal cost.

9. Fireball Company has fixed costs of $318,000. It charges $25.00 for each product and each product's variable cost is $13.00. What is the breakeven point in units?

   (a) 12,720 units
   (b) 26,500 units
   (c) 8,369 units
   (d) 24,462 units

10. The contribution margin ratio is

   (a) the contribution margin expressed as a percentage of sales.
   (b) the contribution margin expressed as a percentage of fixed costs.
   (c) the contribution margin expressed as a percentage of total support costs.
   (d) the contribution margin expressed as a percentage of variable costs.

Completion

1. Total variable costs change in ____________ to changes in the level of production.

2. Economists often represent total costs as an inverted ___-______ curve.

3. Step fixed costs are those that increase in relatively ________ discrete steps.

4. One way to think of Varible costs is that they represent resources whose consumption can be adjusted to match the demand for them.

5. Diseconomy of Scale describes a situation in which average costs increase with increases in production volume.

6. Cost Behavior describes the way costs change with changes in activity cost drivers or with production volume.

7. Support activity resources may be flexable, discretionary, or committed.

8. In the relevant range, Total cost = Fixed cost + Varible cost per unit multiplied by production level in units.

9. At the breakeven point, total Sales Revenue equals total costs.

10. The contribution margin expressed as a Percentage of Sales is referred to as the contribution margin ratio.

Problems

1. The Chow Company budgets sales revenue at $5,000,000, variable costs at $2,500,000 and fixed costs at $1,750,000 for 1997.

   (a) Compute Chow Company's contribution margin ratio.

   5,000,000 − 2,500,000 / 5,000,000 = .50 (50%

   (b) What sales revenue must it generate to break even?

   1.7/.50

   1,750,000 / .50 = 3,500,000

(c) What sales revenue must it generate to earn a target profit of 1,500,000?

1,750,000 + 1,500,000 / .50

= 6.5 mil

(d) What sales revenue must it generate to attain a profit-to-sales ratio of 25%?

2. The Baxter Company manufactures and sells small toys to be put into cereal boxes. Price and cost data for Baxter's operations are:

Costs per 100 Toys	
Selling price	$50.00
Variable Costs:	
Raw materials	$15.00
Direct labor	12.00
Manufacturing support	8.00
Selling expenses	2.00
Total variable costs per unit	$37.00
Annual fixed costs	
Manufacturing support	$160,000
Selling and administrative	120,000
Total fixed costs	$380,000
Estimated sales volume	500,000 toys

(a) What is Baxter Company's breakeven point?

(b) How many toys must Baxter sell to make a target profit of $175,000?

(c) How many toys must Baxter sell to generate a profit-to-sales ratio of 5%?

SOLUTIONS TO PRACTICE TEST QUESTIONS AND PROBLEMS

True/False

1. False. Total variable costs change with changes in the level of production, while total fixed costs remain the same.

2. False. A mixed cost is composed of both fixed and variable costs.

3. True. This is the definition of economies of scale.

4. False. The relevant range holds for both fixed and variable costs.

5. True. This is the way that step variable costs are defined.

6. True. This is the definition of normal cost.

7. True. These are examples of discretionary costs, which result from strategic and tactical decisions of managers..

8. True. Committed resources (for example, plant facilities) have to be available before demand is known.

9. False. The contribution margin is the difference between unit sales price and unit variable cost.

10. True. This is the definition of the breakeven point.

Multiple-Choice

1. b. *Total* variable costs change with changes in the level of production; variable costs *per unit* do not change with changes in the level of production.

2. a. Fixed cost *per unit volume* decreases when production increases; *total* fixed cost stays the same within the relevant range.

3. d. The total cost is $110 + ($0.04 × 40,000) = $1,710.

4. c. The relevant range in a step function cost curve is restricted to be within a step.

5. a. The normal cost is $45,000/375 = $120 per job.

6. d. The use of discretionary resources (defined as those resulting from strategic and tactical decisions of managers) is not directly related to production volume.

7. b. Committed resources (for example, plant equipment) are made available before their demand is known precisely.

8. c. Cost driver is the correct term.

9. b. The breakeven point (in units) = Fixed costs divided by contribution margin per unit or $318,000/(25.00 - 13.00) = 26,500 units.

10. a. The contribution margin ratio is the contribution margin expressed as a percentage of sales.

Completion

1. proportion
2. S shaped
3. wide
4. variable
5. Diseconomies of scale
6. Cost behavior
7. flexible, committed
8. Variable cost per unit
9. sales revenue
10. percentage of sales

Problems

1. (a) Contribution margin ratio = ($5,000,000 - $2,500,000)/$5,000,000

= 0.50 or 50%

(b) Breakeven revenue = $1,750,000/0.50

= $3,500,000

(c) Sales revenue to earn a target profit of $1,500,000:

= ($1,750,000 + $1,500,000)/0.50

= $6,500,000

(d) Let R = the desired revenue, and recall the contribution margin ratio is 0.50.

Profit-to-sales ratio = (0.50R - $1,750,000)/R = 0.25

0.25R = 0.50R - $1,750,000

R = $1,750,000/0.25 = $7,000,000

2. (a) Baxter Company's breakeven point can be calculated as follows:

$50 - 37 = $13 contribution per 100 toys
Contribution margin per toy = $0.13
Total fixed costs are $380,000
Breakeven point is $380,000/0.13 = 2,923,077 toys

(b) Let X = the number of toys that must be sold in order to earn $175,000

X = ($380,000 + $175,000)/0.13
= 4,269,231 toys

(c) Let Y = the number of toys that must be sold in order to generate a profit-to-sales ratio of 5%, and note that sales revenue per toy is $0.50.

Profit-to-sales ratio = (0.13Y - $380,000)/0.50Y = 0.05

Y = $380,000/0.105 = 3,619,048

Notes and Questions

Chapter 5

Basic Product Costing Systems

CENTRAL FOCUS AND LEARNING OBJECTIVES

After reading this chapter, you will be able to

1. understand how using job bid sheets is effective for estimating product costs in a job order costing system.

2. use cost driver rates to apply support activity costs to products.

3. discuss why using cost systems with multiple cost driver rates gives different estimates of product costs than cost systems with a single rate.

4. evaluate a cost system to understand whether it is likely to distort product costs.

5. explain the importance of recording actual costs and comparing them with estimated costs.

6. understand the relevance of performing an analysis of variances between actual and estimated costs, including first- and second-level variances.

7. appreciate the importance of conversion costs and the measurement of costs in multistage, continuous-processing industries.

8. understand the significance of differences between job order costing and multistage process costing systems.

REVIEW OF KEY TERMS AND CONCEPTS

Learning Objective 1:	Understand how using job bid sheets is effective for estimating product costs in a job order costing system.

I. Job Order Costing Systems

A. A **job order costing system** is a system for estimating costs of products in organizations that produce several different types of products. More specifically, a job order costing system estimates costs of producing products for different jobs required for customer orders.

B. **A job bid sheet** is a format for estimating job costs.

See Exhibit 5-1 for an example of a job bid sheet. Note panels 2 and 3 for standard engineering and industrial engineering specifications.

C. **Job costs** are the total of direct material, direct labor, and support activity costs estimated for, or identified with, a job.

D. **Markup or margin** is the amount of profit added to estimated job costs to arrive at a bid price.

E. The markup rate may be contingent on the **rate of return** that the organization has specified. The rate of return is the ratio of net income to investment, also called return on investment.

Learning Objective 2:	Use cost driver rates to apply support activity costs to products.

Learning Objective 3:	Discuss why using cost systems with multiple cost driver rates gives different estimates of product costs than cost systems with a single rate.

F. Determining cost driver rates and costs has become very important. **Cost pools** are identified categories of costs with a separate rate for each category.

G. The **cost driver rate** is the rate at which support activity costs are applied to individual jobs. It is the ratio of the normal cost for a support activity accumulated in a cost pool to the normal level of the cost driver for the activity. See equation (5-1).

H. Determining a cost driver rate as the budgeted (or actual) cost per unit of the budgeted (or actual) use of that activity results in misleading product costs. The cost driver rate is best computed as shown in equation (5-1).

I. A general principle in selecting the **number of cost pools** is that separate cost pools should be used if the productivity of resources is different and if the pattern of demand varies across products.

Make sure that you understand these concepts before proceeding. A comprehensive illustration of how to evaluate a cost system is provided via the Archie's Auto example. Study this example carefully, paying particular attention to Exhibits 5-3 through 5-7.

The Marymount Electronics review problem illustrates the determination of cost driver rates and the assignment of support costs to jobs.

Learning Objective 4: Evaluate a cost system to understand whether it is likely to distort product costs.

Learning Objective 5: Explain the importance of recording actual costs and comparing them with estimated costs.

II. Recording Actual Job Costs

This section discusses the procedures for recording actual job costs.

A. **A materials requisition note** is a note telling the stores department to issue materials to the shop floor in order to commence production.

B. **Worker time cards** record the hours spent by each worker each day or week on different jobs.

C. A **job cost sheet** is a format for recording actual job costs.

Exhibits 5-9, 5-10, and 5-11 provide examples of each of the documents discussed above.

Learning Objective 6: Understand the relevance of performing an analysis of variances between actual and estimated costs, including first- and second-level variances.

III. Basic Variance Analysis

Variances are differences between actual and estimated costs and are a necessary step for managers who are attempting to understand why a difference occurred.

A. A **first-level variance** is the difference between actual and estimated costs for a cost item, such as direct labor or direct materials.

1. A **favorable variance**, signified by an "F," means that actual costs were less than estimated costs.

2. An **unfavorable variance**, signified by a "U," means that actual costs were greater than estimated costs.

B. **Second-level variances** result from further analysis of a first-level variance.

For instance, direct materials can be broken down into efficiency (usage) and price variances. The formulae for calculating second-level variances are as follows:

1. The **direct materials price variance is:**

$(AP - SP) \times AQ$

where
AP = actual price of materials
SP = estimated or standard price of materials
AQ = actual quantity of materials used

2. The **direct materials usage variance** is:

$$(AQ - SQ) \times SP$$

where
AQ = actual quantity of materials used
SQ = estimated or standard quantity of materials required
SP = estimated or standard price of materials

3. The sum of the price and usage variances is the **total direct material variance**, or actual cost minus estimated cost.

Usage variance + Price variance

$$= (AQ - SQ) \times SP + (AP - SP) \times AQ$$

$$= (AP \times AQ) - (SQ \times SP)$$

4. Note that there are times when *the amount of materials purchased is different from that used.* This is because materials often are purchased in large quantities and stored until needed. Thus, it is common to separate out the material price variance at the time of purchase and charge jobs for materials at their standard prices. See equation (5-5).

Direct labor cost also can be broken down into wage rate and efficiency variances

5. The **wage rate variance** is:

$$(AR - SR) \times AH$$

where
AR = actual wage rate
SR = estimated or standard wage rate
AH = actual number of direct labor hours

6. The **efficiency variance** is:

   $(AH - SH) \times SR$

   where
   AH = actual number of direct labor hours
   SH = estimated or standard number of direct labor hours
   SR = estimated or standard wage rate

7. The sum of the wage rate and efficiency variances is the **total direct labor variance**, or actual cost minus estimated cost.

   Wage rate variance + Efficiency variance

   $= (AH - SH) \times SR + (AR - SR) \times AH$

   $= (AR \times AH) - (SR \times SH)$

Carefully work through Exhibits 5-12 through 5-14 on variance analyses. Do you understand all of the calculations?

Learning Objective 7: Appreciate the importance of conversion costs and the measurement of costs in multistage continuous-processing industries.

Learning Objective 8: Understand the significance of differences between job order costing and multistage process costing systems.

IV. Multistage Process Costing Systems

A **multistage process costing system** is a system for determining product costs in multistage processing industries such as chemicals, basic metals, and pharmaceuticals.

A. With this method the first step is to **assess costs for each stage of the process** and then to assign costs to individual products.

B. A common feature of process costing is that the products that are produced are relatively **homogeneous**.

C. Since costs are measured only at process stages, **cost variances** are determined only at the level of the process stages.

D. **Conversion costs** are costs of production labor and support activities to convert the materials or product at each process stage.

Exhibits 5-16 through 5-19 illustrate process costing. Can you describe the differences between job order and process costing? (See Exhibit 5-15).

The summary example illustrates job costing and computation of cost-based bid prices, as well as variance analysis.

PRACTICE TEST QUESTIONS AND PROBLEMS

True/False

____ 1. A job order costing system is a common method for estimating product costs in the chemicals industry.

____ 2. Standard engineering specifications appear on a job bid sheet.

____ 3. Markup and margin are two different concepts.

____ 4. Determination of cost driver rates based on planned or actual short-term usage produces misleading product costs.

____ 5. An unfavorable variance is one in which actual costs are less than estimated costs.

____ 6. Worker time cards record total hours worked for each worker without reference to the specific jobs on which they work.

____ 7. Material usage and price variances are examples of second-level variances.

____ 8. Efficiency and wage rate variances pertain to direct labor costs.

____ 9. Multistage process costing systems are used in the pharmaceuticals industry.

____ 10. In process costing separate records are kept for individual jobs.

Multiple-Choice

1. Each of the following statements is true about job order costing systems, EXCEPT:

    (a) A job order costing system is a method used for estimating product costs in firms that have several distinct products.
    (b) A job order costing system estimates costs of manufacturing products for different jobs required for customer orders.
    (c) A job order costing system provides the means to estimate costs so that bids can be prepared.
    (d) A job order costing system relies on the concept of conversion costs.

2. From the following information determine a price incorporating a 15% markup on job AR1. For AR1, direct materials are $3,000, direct labor is $2,500, and support activity costs are $4,700.

    (a) $ 6,325
    (b) $ 8,855
    (c) $ 8,280
    (d) $11,730

3. Determine the cost driver rate for cost pool ABC from the following information: The required rate of return is 18%; normal cost of support activities is $8,700, the markup percentage is 12%, and the normal level of the cost driver is 225.

    (a) $ 38.67
    (b) $ 1,044.00
    (c) $48,333.33
    (d) $ 27.00

4. The correct method of determining cost driver rates is

    (a) to use the previous year's actual cost per unit of the activity.
    (b) to estimate the normal cost per unit of the activity level committed.
    (c) to estimate the actual cost per unit of the planned usage level of the activity.
    (d) to estimate the actual cost per unit of the activity level committed.

5. A materials requisition note

   (a) instructs shop floor personnel to request materials from its suppliers.
   (b) informs the customer that materials for use in producing their product has been delayed.
   (c) instructs stores to issue materials to the shop floor to commence production.
   (d) is a note from stores to suppliers to ship more materials.

6. Each of the following is essential to recording actual job costs, EXCEPT

   (a) a materials requisition note.
   (b) a stores department quality check form.
   (c) worker time cards.
   (d) a job cost sheet.

7. The difference between first- and second-level variance analysis is

   (a) the level of disaggregation and detail of analysis.
   (b) that first-level applies to direct materials, while second-level applies to direct labor.
   (c) that second-level applies to direct materials, while first-level applies to direct labor.
   (d) that second-level analysis is less detailed than first-level.

8. Which of the formulae below correctly illustrates the calculation for the efficiency variance for direct labor?

   (a) $(AR - SR) \times AH$
   (b) $(AR - SR) \times SH$
   (c) $(AH - SH) \times AR$
   (d) $(AH - SH) \times SR$

9. The formula for the total cost variance for direct labor cost is

   (a) $(AR \times AH) - (SR \times SH)$.
   (b) $(SR \times AH) - (AR \times SH)$.
   (c) $(AR \times SR) - (AH \times SH)$.
   (d) $(AR \times SH) - (SR \times AH)$.

10. Given the following information, calculate the materials price variance for direct materials: AP = $250, SP = $245; AQ = 20.

(a) $100F
(b) $100U
(c) $230U
(d) $225U

Completion

1. A job bid sheet is a format for ________ ________ costs.

2. The cost driver rate is the ratio of the ________ cost for a support activity to the ________ level of the cost ________ for the activity.

3. A ________ ________ note lists the materials required to commence production.

4. Variance analysis is the difference between ________ and ________ costs.

5. The formula for calculating material usage variances is (AQ - ____) × ____.

6. When materials are purchased in large quantities, it is common to separate out the materials price variance ____ ____ ____ ____ ________

7. Efficiency and wage rate variances are associated with ________ ________ ________

8. In a multistage process costing system the first step is to determine costs for ________ ________ of the process and then assign the costs to products.

9. In process costing settings, the common feature is that the products manufactured are all ________________

10. ________ ________ are the costs of production labor and support activities to convert the materials or product at each process stage.

Problems

1. The MPC Company has stamping and assembly departments. MPC uses a single predetermined cost driver rate based on plantwide direct labor hours. The cost estimates for 1997 are as follows:

	Stamping	Assembly	Total
Manufacturing support	$80,000	$28,000	$108,000
Direct labor hours	4,000	7,000	11,000
Machine-hours	6,000	4,000	10,000

(a) Determine the plantwide (single predetermined) cost driver rate for 1997.

(b) Determine departmental cost driver rates based on machine hours for stamping and direct labor hours for assembly.

2. Ohio Company shows the following information for job MX888:

Actual:

Direct materials used:	9000 lbs. purchased at $2.00 per lb.
Direct labor:	1700 hours at $9.50 per hour
Units produced:	600 units

Standard:

Direct materials:	18 lbs. per unit at $1.80 per lb.
Direct labor:	3 hours per unit at wage rate of $9.00 per hour

(a) Determine the material price and usage variances. (The usage variance is also referred to as a quantity or efficiency variance.)

(b) Determine the direct labor wage rate and efficiency variances.

SOLUTIONS TO PRACTICE TEST QUESTIONS AND PROBLEMS

True/False

1. False. The chemicals industry uses process costing methods, as it is a continuous processing industry.

2. True. Job bid sheets contain standard engineering specifications for the materials required.

3. False. The concepts are interchangeable, and are defined as the amount of profit added to estimated job costs to arrive at a price.

4. True. With such an approach, job costs appear to be higher when demand is lower, and vice versa. A "death spiral" can result if perceived higher costs lead to higher bid prices, causing even lower demand and higher cost driver rates.

5. False. An unfavorable variance arises when actual costs are greater than estimated costs.

6. False. Worker time cards specify hours spent on specific jobs.

7. True. These are second-level variances for direct materials.

8. True. Efficiency and wage rate variances are calculated for direct labor.

9. True. The pharmaceuticals industry uses continuous processing because of the degree of homogeneity among its products.

10. False. In process costing it is unnecessary to keep separate records for individual jobs.

Multiple-Choice

1. d. Job order costing does not rely on the concept of conversion costs.

2. d. Job cost for AR1 is the total of direct materials of $3,000, direct labor of $2,500 and support costs of $4,700, or $10,200. The markup is $10,200 × 15% = $1,530, resulting in a price of $10,200 + 1,530 = $11,730.

3. a. The cost driver rate for cost pool ABC equals the normal cost of support activity/normal level of the cost driver, or $8,700/225 = $38.67.

4. b. The correct method of determining cost driver rates is to estimate the normal cost per unit of the activity level committed.

5. c. A materials requisition note instructs stores to issue materials to the shop floor to commence production.

6. b. Stores department quality check forms (a fictitious form) are not used to record actual job costs.

7. a. The difference between first- and second-level variance analysis is the level of disaggregation and detail of analysis. Second-level variances disaggregate first-level variances.

8. d. The correct formula is: (AH - SH) × SR.

9. a. The correct formula is: (AR × AH) - (SR × SH).

10. b. The materials price variance is (AP - SP) × AQ or ($250 - $245) × 20 = $100U, as actual usage was greater than the estimate.

Completion

1. estimating job
2. normal, normal, driver
3. materials requisition
4. estimated, actual
5. SQ, SP
6. at the time of purchase
7. direct labor costs
8. each stage

9. relatively homogeneous

10. Conversion costs

Problems

1. (a) The plantwide cost driver rate

= \$108,000/11,000 direct labor hours

= \$9.82 per direct labor hour

(b) Departmental cost driver rates:

Stamping Department: = \$80,000/6,000 machine hours

= \$13.34 per machine hour

Assembly Department: = \$28,000/7,000 direct labor hours

= \$4 per direct labor hour

2. (a). Materials price variance = (AP - SP) × AQ

= (\$2.00 - \$1.80) × 9,000

= \$1,800 Unfavorable

Materials quantity variance = (AQ - SQ) × SP

= [9,000 - (18 × 600)] × \$1.80

= \$3,240 Favorable

(b) Direct labor wage rate variance = (AR - SR) × AH

= (\$9.50 - \$9.00) × 1,700

= \$850 Unfavorable

Direct labor efficiency variance = (AH - SH) × SR

= [(1,700 - (3 × 600)] × \$9

= \$900 Favorable

Notes and Questions

Chapter 6

Two-Stage Allocations and Activity-Based Costing Systems

CENTRAL FOCUS AND LEARNING OBJECTIVES

After reading this chapter, you will be able to

1. understand why the difference between production and service departments is important.
2. discuss the importance and method of allocating service department costs to production departments.
3. identify and use the two stages of cost allocations and understand the differences between them.
4. understand why decision-makers should know how conventional two-stage allocation methods often distort production costs.
5. use activity-based costing systems to estimate product costs.
6. assign selling and distribution costs to products.

REVIEW OF KEY TERMS AND CONCEPTS

Learning Objective 1: Understand why the difference between production and service departments is important.

I. The Two-Stage Cost Allocation Method

This section discusses conventional methods of allocation and begins with a discussion of how departmental structure affects allocation methods.

A. Effects of Departmental Structure on Allocation

Many plants are organized into departments that perform designated activities.

1. **Production departments** are those directly responsible for some of the work of converting raw materials into finished products. Examples include casting, stamping, machining, assembly, and packing departments.

2. **Service departments** are those performing activities that support production, but are not responsible for any of the conversion stages. Examples include machine maintenance, machine setup, and production scheduling. All service department costs are indirect support activity costs (with respect to products) because they do not arise from direct production activities.

Study Exhibit 6-1 carefully, as it forms the basis for the rest of the discussion in this chapter.

Learning Objective 2: Discuss the importance and method of allocating service department costs to production departments.

Learning Objective 3: Identify and use the two stages of cost allocations and understand the differences between them.

B. The Two-Stage Method

1. Conventional product costing systems assign indirect costs to products or jobs in two stages.

2. Step 1 of **Stage 1** identifies or estimates the normal manufacturing support costs (indirect costs) incurred in each production and service department. Step 2 of **Stage 1** then allocates all service department costs to the production departments.

   a. **The direct allocation method** is a simple method to allocate service department costs to production departments. This method ignores interdependencies between service departments.

Follow the Medequip example to understand Stage 1 cost allocations. Exhibits 6-2 through 6-6 illustrate the process.

   b. **The sequential allocation method** is a method that recognizes interdependencies between service departments and allocates service department costs, one service department at a time, in sequential order. See Appendix 6-1 for more details on this method.

   c. **The reciprocal allocation method** is a method to determine service department cost allocations simultaneously, recognizing the reciprocity between pairs of service departments. See Appendix 6-1 for details on this method.

3. In **Stage 2,** the system assigns all of the accumulated indirect costs for the production department to individual products or jobs, based on predetermined cost driver rates. The allocation bases for production departments often are unit-based

measures and include the number of units produced, the number of direct labor hours, direct labor cost, and the number of machine hours.

Stage 2 allocations are illustrated in the Medequip example in Exhibits 6-7 through 6-11.

Learning Objective 4: Understand why decision-makers should know how conventional two-stage allocation methods often distort production costs.

II. Distortions Caused by Two-Stage Allocations

There are two major reasons why two-stage allocations can distort product costs.

A. Allocations are based on unit-related measures.

B. Consumption ratios of resources for products often are different from those based on unit-related measures.

For example, a distortion can arise if a unit-related measure such as machine hours is used for cost allocation even though some products are produced in larger batches requiring fewer setup costs, and thus consume differential amounts of support costs. Note in Exhibit 6-11 that A is produced in larger batch sizes than B is. Because the two products require the same number of machine hours, both A and B will be allocated the same support costs, even though B requires more setups.

The review problem illustrates the assignment of costs to jobs and products using the two-stage allocation method.

Learning Objective 5: Use activity-based costing systems to estimate product costs.

III. Activity-Based Costing Systems

A. Product-cost distortions resulting from conventional two-stage systems can be overcome by designing a costing system that uses the actual cost driver for each activity to assign costs directly to products. This kind of system is called an activity-based costing system.

Activity-based costing is an extremely important method that has changed the way many decision-makers think about management accounting. Carefully work through Exhibits 6-12 through 6-15.

B. **Activity-based costing systems** are costing systems based on cost drivers that link activities performed to products and allocate support activity costs directly to products using these cost drivers.

Do you now know the differences between two-stage allocation methods and activity-based costing? How does activity-based costing overcome the distortions caused by the two-stage method?

Learning Objective 6: Assign selling and distribution costs to products.

IV. Selling and Distribution Activities

Many organizations are realizing the importance of linking selling and distribution costs more carefully to products and customers.

A. Many conventional systems either completely exclude selling and distribution and other nonmanufacturing costs from product costs or use arbitrary methods such as relative sales value to assign them.

B. Today, because of the new emphasis on customer orientation and technological innovation for competitive advantage, selling and distribution costs are being examined more closely. The general idea is to determine whether some products require greater selling and distribution costs than others, and to determine whether some of these costs should be included in product costs.

Exhibits 6-16 through 6-18 illustrate how selling and distribution costs can be analyzed from an activity-based costing viewpoint. Study these exhibits carefully.

V. Appendix 6-1

A. The Sequential Allocation Method

1. The **sequential method of allocation** is used if no two service departments consume a significant proportion of the services produced by the other department.

2. Under this method, the service departments are arranged in order so that a service department can receive costs allocated from another service department only before its own costs are allocated to other departments.

3. The costs of the service department that provides the highest percentage of its service to other service departments are allocated first. This procedure continues, with the department providing the lowest percentage of its service going last. Once a service department's costs are allocated, no costs of any other department can be allocated back to it.

4. The total costs of service departments allocated to other departments are the directly identified costs with that department plus the amount(s) allocated earlier from other service departments.

See Exhibits 6-21 and 6-22 for an illustration of the sequential allocation method.

B. The Reciprocal Allocation Method

1. When there are interactions between different service departments (e.g., when both provide service to each other), the **reciprocal method** is used.

2. The sequential method cannot work in this situation because allocating the service costs of department A to B, both of which provide service to each other, means that B will then have to allocate a portion of A's cost back to it. This cannot work because all of A's costs have already been allocated. Thus, A would still have unallocated costs in it.

3. Solving this problem requires using simultaneous equations, as shown in the text.

Carefully work through equations (6-1) and (6-2) in the text on reciprocal allocation, and Exhibits 6-23 and 6-24 for an illustration of the reciprocal allocation method.

PRACTICE TEST QUESTIONS AND PROBLEMS

True/False

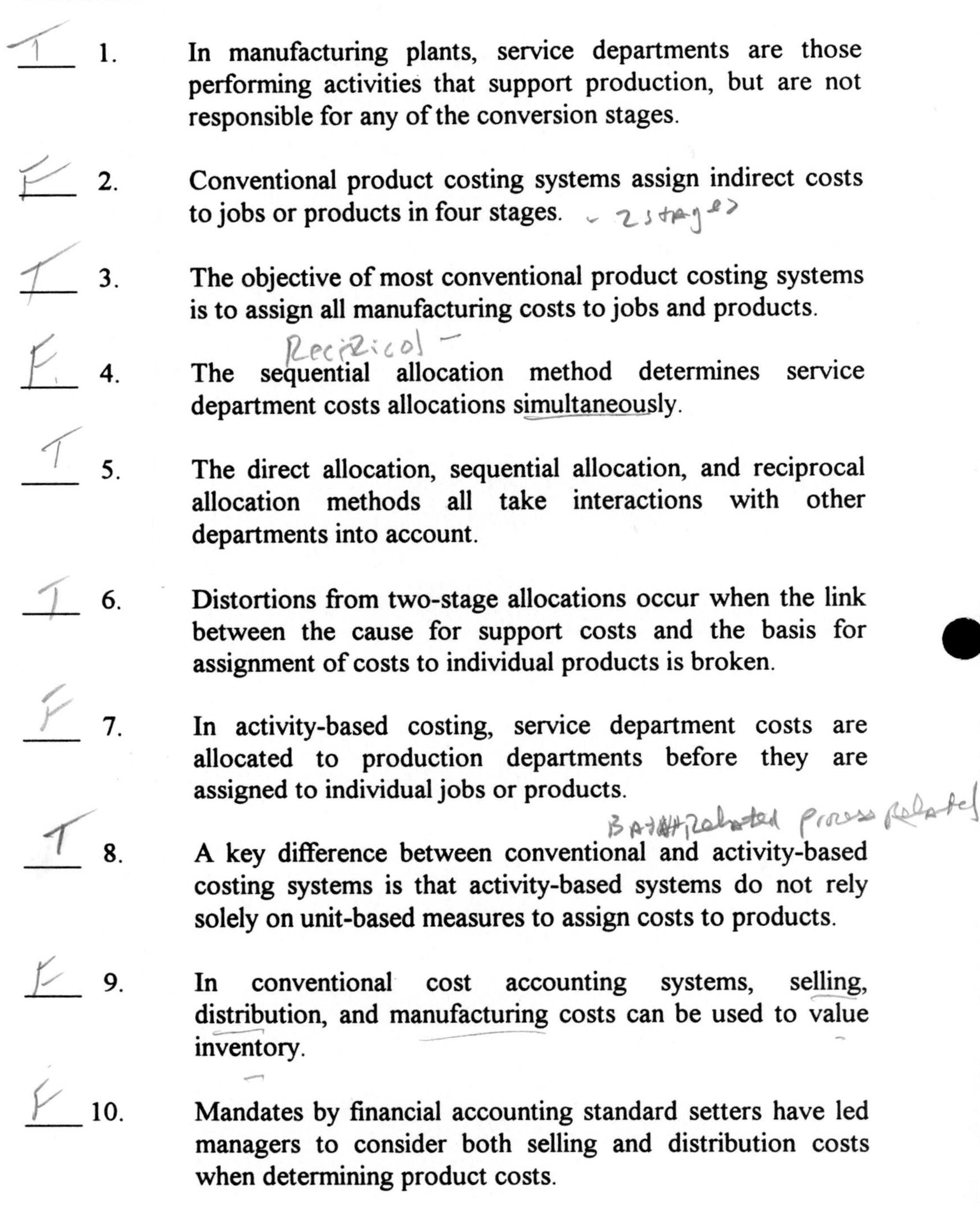

____ 1. In manufacturing plants, service departments are those performing activities that support production, but are not responsible for any of the conversion stages.

____ 2. Conventional product costing systems assign indirect costs to jobs or products in four stages.

____ 3. The objective of most conventional product costing systems is to assign all manufacturing costs to jobs and products.

____ 4. The sequential allocation method determines service department costs allocations simultaneously.

____ 5. The direct allocation, sequential allocation, and reciprocal allocation methods all take interactions with other departments into account.

____ 6. Distortions from two-stage allocations occur when the link between the cause for support costs and the basis for assignment of costs to individual products is broken.

____ 7. In activity-based costing, service department costs are allocated to production departments before they are assigned to individual jobs or products.

____ 8. A key difference between conventional and activity-based costing systems is that activity-based systems do not rely solely on unit-based measures to assign costs to products.

____ 9. In conventional cost accounting systems, selling, distribution, and manufacturing costs can be used to value inventory.

____ 10. Mandates by financial accounting standard setters have led managers to consider both selling and distribution costs when determining product costs.

Multiple-Choice

1. In stage one of the conventional cost allocation procedure, the first step is to

   (a) assess actual support costs for each department.
   (b) estimate normal support costs for each department.
   (c) allocate all service department support costs to production departments.
   (d) allocate production department costs to individual products.

2. Satellite Company has total support costs of $480,000. It uses a conventional cost accounting system and has 5 service departments and 5 production departments which produce 25 different products. Ultimately, how much of the $480,000 will NOT be allocated down to the product level?

   (a) $ 48,000
   (b) $480,000
   (c) $ 1,920
   (d) $ 0

3. Below are four activities and four allocation bases. Which of the four has the weakest link between activity and allocation basis?

	Activity	Allocation Basis
(a)	Machine maintenance	Square feet of floor space
(b)	Lighting on shop floor	Number of kilowatt hours
(c)	Quality control	Number of inspections
(d)	Ordering of materials	Number of orders

4. Unit-related measures include all of the following, EXCEPT

   (a) number of units made.
   (b) number of direct labor hours.
   (c) number of machine hours.
   (d) number of material handlers.

5. Products MX518 and MX536 each are assigned $25.00 in support costs by a conventional accounting system. An activity analysis revealed that although subsequent production requirements are identical, MX518 requires 30 minutes more setup time than MX536. According to an activity-based costing system, MX518 is ________________ under the conventional accounting system.

   (a) undercosted
   (b) overcosted
   (c) fairly costed
   (d) accurately costed

6. Activity-based costing develops cost drivers that

   (a) do not take any support activities into account.
   (b) take only some production activities into account.
   (c) directly link the activities performed to the products produced.
   (d) indirectly link the activities performed to the products produced.

7. Archer Company produces six products. Under their conventional method of cost allocation, using one cost driver, job AR6 costs $142.75. Activity-based costing was applied to all of Archer's products, and three cost drivers were found to be necessary. The new cost of AR6 was determined to be $133.00. Given this change in the cost of AR6, which of the following statements regarding product AR6 under activity-based costing is the most accurate?

   (a) AR6 is less accurately costed.
   (b) AR6 is more accurately costed.
   (c) AR6 will now command a much higher sales price.
   (d) AR6 will now command a much lower sales price.

8. In question 7 above, for Archer Company, the total amount of support cost to be allocated under the conventional method is ____________ the total amount under the activity-based costing method.

   (a) less than
   (b) slightly more than
   (c) identical to
   (d) much more than

9. Which of the following is not a selling or distribution cost?

   (a) Order execution
   (b) Shipping
   (c) Sales catalog
   (d) Material purchasing

10. A key reason for including selling and distribution costs in product costing is that

   (a) the demand for the selling and distribution activities placed by different products for different customers needs to be reflected.
   (b) generally accepted accounting principles now require it.
   (c) customers have demanded it.
   (d) controllers have demanded it.

Completion

1. All service department costs are __________ costs of products because they do not arise from direct production activities.

2. Conventional costing systems assume that we cannot obtain __________ measures of the use of service departments' resources on individual jobs as conveniently as we can for production departments.

3. The second step in Stage 1 of the cost allocation procedure involves allocating ______________ ______________ costs to ______________ ________________.

4. Stage 2 allocations require the identification of appropriate __________ __________ for each production department.

5. The __________ ___________ method is a simple method that allocates the service department costs directly to the production departments, ignoring interactions among other departments.

6. Two related factors contribute to distortions from the two-stage allocation procedure. The first is that allocations are based on unit-related measures, and the second is differences in __________ ___________ ___________.

7. Two-stage allocation distortions can be eliminated if costing systems are designed that use the ____________ cost drivers for each support activity to assign costs _____________ to products.

8. Analysis of sales support activities can provide useful insights about differences in the cost of sales and marketing activity resources consumed by different _____________ ____________, ________ ___ _______________, or ____________ _____________.

9. With conventional costing systems, products manufactured in ________ batches or in ________ annual volumes may be undercosted because batch-related and product-sustaining costs are assigned using unit-related drivers.

10. In the past, conventional cost systems either completely excluded selling and distribution costs or assigned them to products on an ____________ basis.

Problems

1. Determine a cost driver for each of the following activities:

   (a) Electricity

   (b) Purchasing

   (c) Equipment setups

   (d) Computer services

   (e) Plant depreciation

   (f) Janitorial service

   (g) Quality assurance

   (h) Administrative services

   (i) Shipping

   (j) Robot maintenance

2. ABKY company has determined the following information about support cost pools and cost drivers:

Cost Pool	Activity Costs	Cost Drivers
Machine setups	$250,000	4,000 setup hours
Material handling	80,000	25,000 lbs. of material
Inspection	30,000	2,000 inspections

The following information pertains to the manufacturing of Products TM3 and MP179:

	TM3	MP179
Number of units produced	3,000	5,000
Direct materials	$24,000	$32,000
Direct labor	$14,000	$18,000
Number of setup hours	100	120
Pounds of material used	3,000	4,500
Number of inspections	20	15

Determine the unit cost for each of the two products using an activity-based costing approach.

SOLUTIONS TO PRACTICE TEST QUESTIONS AND PROBLEMS

True/False

1. True. This is the definition of service departments in manufacturing plants.

2. False. Conventional product costing systems assign indirect costs to jobs or products in two stages.

3. True. This is the objective of most conventional product costing systems.

4. False. The reciprocal allocation method considers service department cost allocations simultaneously.

5. False. The direct allocation method does not take interactions with other departments into account.

6. True. When this link breaks, distortions occur.

7. False. In activity-based costing this step is bypassed as activities are directly linked to products.

8. True. Activity-based systems also rely on batch-related and product-sustaining measures.

9. False. In conventional systems only manufacturing costs can be used to value inventory.

10. False. Financial standard setters are not involved. Rather, a more intense customer orientation and technological innovation are causing greater focus on selling and distribution costs required to provide products to customers.

Multiple-Choice

1. b. The first step is to estimate normal support costs for each department.

2. d. All of the $480,000 will be allocated down to the product level.

3. a. The weakest link is between machine maintenance and floor space.

4. d. The number of material handlers is not a unit-related measure.

5. a. MX518 is undercosted, as it is actually consuming more resources than represented by its cost allocation.

6. c. ABC develops cost drivers that directly link the activities performed to the products produced.

7. b. Product AR6 is now more accurately costed, given the use of three cost drivers and the activity-based costing method.

8. c. The total amount of support cost to be allocated is identical under both systems, but the relative costs of each job are likely to change, based on the new cost drivers.

9. d. Materials purchasing is not a selling or distribution cost.

10. a. The demand for the selling and distribution activities needs to be reflected in product costs for managerial purposes.

Completion

1. indirect
2. direct
3. service department, production departments
4. allocation bases (or cost drivers)
5. direct allocation
6. relative consumption rates
7. actual, directly
8. product lines, types of customers, market segments
9. small, small
10. arbitrary

Problems

1. (a) Number of kilowatt hours
   (b) Number of orders
   (c) Number of setup hours
   (d) Number of hours of service provided
   (e) Number of square feet
   (f) Number of square feet
   (g) Number of inspections
   (h) Number of employees
   (i) Number of shipments
   (j) Number of robot hours

2.

Cost Pool	Activity Costs	Cost Drivers	Driver Rates
Machine setups	$250,000	4,000 hrs.	$62.50/hr
Material handling	80,000	25,000 lbs.	$ 3.20/lb.
Inspection	30,000	2,000 insp.	$15.00/insp.

		TM3	MP179
Direct materials		$24,000	$33,000
Direct labor		14,000	18,000
Support costs:			
Machine setups	[$62.50 * 100 (120)]	6,250	7,500
Materials handling	[$3.2 * 3,000 (4500)]	9,600	14,400
Inspection	[$15 * 20 (15)]	300	225
Total manufacturing costs		$54,150	$72,125
Number of units produced		3,000	5,000
Unit cost		$18.05	$14.43

Notes and Questions

Chapter 7

Pricing and Product-Mix Decisions

CENTRAL FOCUS AND LEARNING OBJECTIVES

After reading this chapter, you will be able to

1. understand the way a firm chooses its product mix in the short term in response to prices set in the market for its products.

2. explain the way a firm adjusts its prices in the short term depending on whether capacity is limited.

3. discuss the way a firm determines a long-term benchmark price to guide its pricing strategy.

4. discuss the way a firm evaluates the long-term profitability of its products and market segments.

REVIEW OF KEY TERMS AND CONCEPTS

Learning Objective 1:	Understand the way a firm chooses its product mix in the short term in response to prices set in the market for its products.

I. Role of Product Costs in Pricing and Product Mix Decisions

A. Understanding how product costs should be analyzed is extremely important for **pricing decisions** when a firm can set or influence the prices of its products.

B. Product cost analysis is also important if prices are set by market forces. The firm can use product cost analysis in deciding the **product mix** to produce and sell.

C. With respect to the ability to influence market prices, there are two general types of firms, price takers and price setters.

1. A **price-taker firm** is one that has little or no influence on the industry supply-and-demand forces, and, consequently, on the prices of its products.

2. A **price-setter firm** is one that sets or bids the prices of its products because it enjoys a significant market share in its industry segment.

II. Short- and Long-Run Pricing Decisions

A. Many resources committed to activities are more than likely fixed in the short run, as capacities cannot be easily altered.

B. In the short run, special attention must be paid to the time period over which capacity is committed, as commitments may constrain the firm and not allow it to seek more profitable opportunities.

C. If production is constrained by inadequate capacity, overtime or the use of subcontractors can help augment capacity in the short run.

D. In the long run, managers have more flexibility in adjusting the capacities of activity resources to match demand for resources.

E. Whether the firm is a price-taker or price-setter is also important.

III. Short-Run Product Mix Decisions

A. Small firms who are price takers can have little influence on the overall industry supply and demand and thus, little influence on the prices of its products. Small firms cannot demand a higher price for their products, as customers may go elsewhere. If a small firm tries to lower prices below industry prices, large firms might retaliate by engaging in a price war which would make the small firm and the industry worse off.

B. The simple decision rule for a price-taker firm is *to sell as many of its products as possible as long as their costs are less than their prices.* But two considerations must be kept in mind:

1. What costs are **relevant** to the short-run product mix decision? Should all product costs be included or only those that vary in the short run?

2. Managers may not be able to produce and sell more of those products whose costs are less than their prices given capacity constraints. In other words, how **flexible** are the capacities of the firm's activity resources?

Exhibits 7-2 through 7-7 on the Texcel Company provide a comprehensive example of short-run product mix decisions. Work through this example carefully.

3. The Texcel example illustrates a key point: the criterion used to decide which products are the most profitable to produce and sell at prevailing prices is the **contribution margin per unit of the constrained resource** (which was machine hours in this example).

IV. The Impact of Opportunity Costs

A variation in the Texcel problem discussed above is a situation in which a decision-maker chooses one alternative over another. Thus, an opportunity cost arises.

A. An **opportunity cost** is the potential benefit sacrificed, when, in selecting one alternative, another alternative is given up. In the Texcel example, if the company accepts the order of 2,000 shirts from the new customer (the selected alternative), then Texcel must give up production of some garments it is currently producing and selling. The opportunity cost in this case is the lost profit on the garments that can no longer be made and sold.

B. In the Texcel example, if Texcel accepts the new order, it should sacrifice production of the garment(s) with the **lowest contribution margin per unit of the constrained resource.** That is, it should sacrifice the garment(s) that lead to **minimization of the opportunity cost.** Texcel's price per unit of the new order should result in at least as much contribution margin per machine hour as Texcel must sacrifice from lost sales of current garments.

Learning Objective 2: Explain the way a firm adjusts its prices in the short term depending on whether capacity is limited.

V. Short-Run Pricing Decisions

A. The **full costs** for a job are the sum of all costs (direct materials, direct labor, and support activity costs) assigned to the job.

B. This section discusses the relationship between costs and prices bid by a supplier for special orders that do not involve long-term relationships with the customer. Two cases are discussed: when there is available surplus capacity and no available surplus capacity.

Work through the Chaney Tools and Dies Company example in Exhibit 7-8.

1. Available Surplus Capacity

    a. **Incremental costs** (or revenues) are the amount by which costs (or revenues) increase if one particular alternative is chosen instead of another.

    b. When sufficient capacity is available, the minimum acceptable price must at least cover the incremental costs to produce and deliver the order. Briefly, incremental revenues must be greater than incremental costs.

2. No Available Surplus Capacity

    a. When there is no available capacity, a firm will have to incur costs to acquire the necessary capacity. This may mean operating the plant on an overtime basis.

    b. Again, the decision rule is that incremental revenues must be greater than incremental costs. In this case, however, incremental costs will be higher than when surplus capacity is available.

C. **Relevant costs** (or revenues) are the costs (or revenues) that differ across alternatives, and, therefore, must be considered in deciding which alternative is the best. Incremental costs are the relevant costs for the kinds of short-run decisions discussed above.

The review problem on Prime Printer illustrates short-term pricing and mix decisions.

Learning Objective 3: Discuss the way a firm determines a long-term benchmark price to guide its pricing strategy.

VI. Long-Run Pricing Decisions

A. Relevant costs for short-run special order pricing decisions differ from full costs. What is the benefit of having full cost information?

B. Reliance on full costs for pricing can be economically justified in three types of situations:

1. Government contracts and pricing in regulated industries (such as electric utilities) that specify prices as full costs with a markup.

2. Over the long term, managers have greater flexibility in adjusting the level of commitment for all activity resources. Thus, full costs are relevant for long-run pricing decisions.

3. Because of short-run fluctuations in the demand for products, firms adjust their prices up and down over a period of time. Over the long run, their average prices tend to equal the price based on full costs that may be set in a long-term contract.

C. The amount of markup is contingent on several factors:

1. If the **strength of demand** for the product is high, a higher markup can be used.

2. If **demand is elastic**, a small increase in price results in a large decrease in demand. Markups are lower when demand is elastic.

3. When **competition is intense,** markups decrease, as it is hard for firms to sustain prices much higher than their incremental costs.

4. Markups may be purposefully lowered based on firm strategy. Two types of strategies are:

   a. A **skimming price strategy**, which involves charging a higher price initially from customers willing to pay more for the privilege of possessing a new product.

b. A **penetration pricing strategy**, which is charging a lower price initially to win market share from an established product of a competing firm.

Learning Objective 4: Discuss the way a firm evaluates the long-term profitability of its products and market segments.

VII. Long-Run Mix Decisions

A. Decisions to add new, or drop existing, products from the product portfolio often have long-term implications for the cost structure of the firm.

B. Resources committed for batch-related and product-sustaining activities cannot be easily changed in the short run, so the mix cannot be changed quickly.

C. Another consideration is that, in some cases, customers may desire a firm to maintain a full product line so that they do not have to go elsewhere. Thus, some unprofitable products may have be kept to maintain the entire product line. If this is too costly, managers might try methods such as re-engineering to lower the cost of some products.

D. One caveat is that dropping products will help profitability only if managers also eliminate, or redeploy, the activity resources no longer required to support the dropped product.

Do you understand the key features of long-term pricing and mix decisions?

The summary example on Faxtronics reviews some important points from this chapter.

VIII. Appendix 7-1

A. The objective of the Appendix is to present an economic analysis of the pricing decision. Note that a knowledge of basic differential calculus is need to work through the examples.

B. The quantity choice is examined and presented in terms of equating marginal revenue and marginal cost. **Marginal revenue** (or cost) is the increase in revenue (or cost) corresponding to a unit increase in the quantity produced and sold.

Carefully work through the examples and study the graph in Exhibit 7-10.

PRACTICE TEST QUESTIONS AND PROBLEMS

True/False

____ 1. An important function of management accountants is to supply cost information so that managers can make product pricing and mix decisions.

____ 2. In the short run, managers have a great deal of flexibility in adjusting the capacities of resources to match the demand for these resources.

____ 3. Firms in industries in which products are highly customized are often price setters.

____ 4. The key criterion to use in short-term product mix decisions when deciding which products are the most profitable to produce and sell at current prices is the contribution margin per unit of constrained resource.

____ 5. Full costs can never be used for pricing.

____ 6. The elasticity of demand has a direct effect on markups.

____ 7. A penetration pricing strategy involves a firm choosing to use a low markup for a new product.

____ 8. Resources committed for product-sustaining activities can be easily changed in the short run.

____ 9. A firm may choose to keep an unprofitable product in order to offer a full product line.

____ 10. Dropping products will always improve profitability.

Multiple-Choice

1. Short-run pricing decisions depend on all of the following, EXCEPT

   (a) whether surplus capacity is available for additional production.
   (b) whether the available capacity limits production.
   (c) the time period of the contract over which capacity is committed.
   (d) the level of product-sustaining activities and costs.

2. A small firm on the fringe of an industry is probably

   (a) a price setter.
   (b) a price taker.
   (c) both a price taker and a price setter.
   (d) a price maker.

3. Cherilee Company produces two products, AR4 and AR8. AR4 has a contribution per unit of $3.00 and requires .3 machine hours per unit, while AR8 has a contribution of $2.50 and requires .2 machine hours per unit. The company's policy is to sell only products with a contribution per unit of constrained resource greater than $9.90. What should they do?

   (a) Sell both AR4 and AR8.
   (b) Sell only AR4.
   (c) Sell only AR8.
   (d) Sell neither AR4 nor AR8.

4. An opportunity cost is

   (a) completely intangible and not measurable.
   (b) the sacrificed potential benefit of choosing one alternative over another.
   (c) the sacrificed past benefit of choosing one alternative over another.
   (d) not relevant to any decision.

5. Lido Company manufactures product MY40. Currently, the product sells for $55, with total costs to manufacture equaling $30. In order to add a new feature to the product, additional direct materials of $3.00, direct labor of $2.50, and batch-related costs of $1.45 per unit would have to be incurred. What are the incremental costs per unit of the decision to add the new feature?

   (a) $3.00
   (b) $2.50
   (c) $6.95
   (d) $5.50

6. Full cost pricing can be economically justified under the following circumstances, EXCEPT

   (a) when customized products are produced.
   (b) when contracts are developed with governmental agencies.
   (c) when a firm enters into a long-term contractual relationship with a customer to supply a product.
   (d) when a firm enters into a short-term contractual relationship with a customer to supply a product.

7. Markups are least affected by

   (a) sudden changes in technology.
   (b) elasticity of demand.
   (c) intensity of competition.
   (d) strength of demand.

8. Demand is elastic when

   (a) a small increase in price results in a small decrease in demand.
   (b) price increases cause demand to fluctuate wildly.
   (c) a small increase in price results in a large decrease in demand.
   (d) price increases cause demand to increase.

9. Which of the following strategies to reduce the cost of a product is the least effective?

   (a) Re-engineer the product.
   (b) Reduce the number of features of the product.
   (c) Offer customers incentives to increase order sizes.
   (d) Improve production processes to reduce setup time.

10. For long-run product mix decisions, managers rely on the _________ costs of the products. That is, managers rely on the costs that reflect the consumption of different activity resources for the manufacture and sale of different products.

    (a) variable
    (b) opportunity
    (c) incremental
    (d) normal

Completion

1. Even when prices are set by overall market supply and demand forces, and the firm has little influence on product prices, managers use cost information to decide the _____ of products to _________ and ______ given their market prices.

2. Decisions to introduce new products or eliminate existing ones have _____-____ consequences, and our emphasis in analyzing such decisions is on the demand each product places on _____________ _____________.

3. A small firm, or a firm with a negligible market share behaves as a _________ _________.

4. The contribution margin, or contribution from each of the firm's products to the firm's profits, is determined by subtracting the _____________ __________ from the price of the product.

5. Giving up the production of a profitable product for another results in an _______________ cost.

6. The ________ costs of a product are the sum of direct materials, direct labor, and support costs.

7. _____________ costs are defined as the amount by which costs increase if one particular decision is made instead of another.

8. _____________ costs are defined as the costs that must be considered in deciding which alternative is best.

9. A supplier bidding on special orders that do not involve long-term relationships with the customer should compare _____________ ____________ to _______________ __________.

10. When a ____________ pricing strategy is used, a higher price is charged to customers willing to pay for the privilege of possessing the latest technological innovations.

Problems

1. Plasticraft Company produces and sells a single product called a DROID. Plasticraft has excess capacity to manufacture 5,000 additional DROIDS. Variable costs are $35 per unit, and fixed costs total $300,000 per month. Ajax Company has offered to pay Plasticraft $39 per unit for a one-time special order for 4,000 DROIDS. This special order requires some additional selling expenses of $1.50 per unit. Should Plasticraft accept this special order?

2. Superior Company produces two porcelain figurines of Lucy and Linus. The selling prices and variable costs for each figurine are as follows:

	Linus	Lucy
Selling price	$25.00	$20.00
Variable costs:		
Direct materials	9.00	6.00
Direct labor	5.00	2.00
Support	4.00	2.00

The cost of direct labor is $10.00 per hour and only 500 hours of labor time are available each week.

(a) Determine the contribution margin per direct labor hour for each product.

(b) Which product should Superior's sales force promote?

SOLUTIONS TO PRACTICE TEST QUESTIONS AND PROBLEMS

True/False

1. True. This is a critical function of the management accountant.

2. False. In the short run, managers have little flexibility in adjusting the capacities of resources.

3. True. Such firms are often price setters.

4. True. The contribution per unit of constrained resource is the key concept.

5. False. There are a number of instances in which full costs can be used, such as government contracting.

6. True. The elasticity of demand has a direct effect on markups.

7. True. This is the definition of a penetration strategy.

8. False. Resources committed for product-sustaining activities cannot easily be changed in the short run.

9. True. In the short run, the firm may feel compelled to offer a full line of products. If the cost of one particular product is so high that it is unreasonable to keep the product, the firm must think of ways to phase it out and substitute different products for the customer.

10. False. Dropping products will improve profitability only if managers eliminate or redeploy the activity resources no longer required to support the product.

Multiple-Choice

1. d. The level of product-sustaining activities and costs are more relevant for long-run decisions.

2. b. Such firms are usually price takers.

3. a. Both AR4 and AR8 have contributions per unit of constrained resource (machine hours) greater than \$9.90: AR4's is \$10.00 and AR8's is \$12.50. Thus, both AR4 and AR8 should be sold.

4. b. An opportunity cost is the sacrificed potential benefit of choosing one alternative over another.

5. c. The incremental costs are the sum of the additional direct materials, direct labor, and batch-related costs, or \$6.95.

6. d. Full cost pricing is not justified when a firm enters into a short-term contractual relationship with a customer to supply a product.

7. a. Markups are least affected by sudden changes in technology.

8. c. Demand is elastic when small increases in price cause large decreases in demand.

9. b. The least effective strategy is to reduce the number of features of the product. While this may reduce costs, it could make the product less appealing to customers.

10. d. For long-run product mix decisions, managers rely on the normal costs of the products. That is, managers rely on the costs that reflect the consumption of different activity resources for the manufacture and sale of different products.

Completion

1. mix, manufacture, sell

2. long run, activity resources

3. price taker

4. variable costs

5. opportunity

6. full

7. Incremental

8. Relevant

9. incremental revenue, incremental cost

10. skimming

Problems

1. Yes, Plasticraft should accept Ajax Company's offer, as it will increase its operating income by $10,000 = [$39 - ($35 + $1.50)] × 4,000 DROIDS.

2. (a) Contribution margin per direct labor hour for each product:

	Linus	Lucy
Selling price	$25.00	$20.00
Less:		
Variable costs		
Direct materials	9.00	6.00
Direct labor	5.00	2.00
Support	4.00	2.00
Contribution margin per figurine	$ 7.00	$10.00
Direct labor hours per figurine	0.5 (5/10)	0.2 (2/10)
Contribution margin per direct labor hour	$14.00	$50.00

(b) Superior's sales force should promote the Lucy figurine, as it has the higher contribution margin per unit of constrained resource (direct labor hours).

Notes and Questions

Chapter 8

Process and Activity Decisions

CENTRAL FOCUS AND LEARNING OBJECTIVES

After reading this chapter, you will be able to

1. understand why sunk costs are not relevant costs.
2. analyze make-or-buy decisions.
3. understand the influence of qualitative factors on the quantitative analysis of decisions.
4. describe the different types of facilities layouts.
5. explain the purpose of just-in-time manufacturing systems.
6. describe the cost savings resulting from reductions in inventories, reduction in production cycle time, production yield improvements, and reductions in rework and defect rates.

REVIEW OF KEY TERMS AND CONCEPTS

Learning Objective 1: Understand why sunk costs are not relevant costs.

I. Monetary Implications and Relevant Costs

A. Managers must evaluate the monetary implications of decisions, and the appropriate tradeoffs between costs and benefits resulting from different alternatives. The key question is: Which costs and revenues are relevant for decision-making?

B. **Relevant revenues and costs** are those that differ across decision alternatives; designation as relevant depends on the decision context and the alternatives available.

C. **Sunk costs** are costs of resources that have already been committed, and, regardless of what decision managers make, these costs cannot be avoided. *Sunk costs are not considered relevant costs.*

Carefully work through the Bonner Company example on relevant costs for the decision to purchase a new machine. Note that the purchase price of the old machine and the payments that must be made on it are sunk costs and not relevant for the decision. Further, Exhibit 8-2 illustrates that the relevant cash outflows and inflows.

Learning Objective 2: Analyze make-or-buy decisions.

II. Make-or-Buy Decisions

The **make-or-buy decision** is to either make a part or component in-house or source it from an outside supplier.

A. **Outsourcing** is purchasing a product, part, or component from an outside supplier instead of manufacturing it in-house.

B. **Avoidable costs** are those that are eliminated when a part, a product, a product line, or a business segment is discontinued.

Learning Objective 3: Understand the influence of qualitative factors on the quantitative analysis of decisions.

C. **Qualitative factors,** such as the reputation of a supplier, can help influence quantitative decisions. Factors such as the supplier's ability to meet performance standards on time are critical to success. Some businesses have chosen to certify suppliers. A **certified supplier** is a specially selected supplier who is assured a high level of business for conforming to high standards for quality and delivery schedules.

Study Exhibit 8-3 on the make-or-buy decision.

Learning Objective 4: Describe the different types of facilities layouts.

III. Facilities Layout Systems

A. **Cycle time** is the total time the organization needs to complete a sequence of activities, or cycle. There are four types of activities which when summed together give total cycle time. As nonvalue-added activities related to these decrease, cycle time and costs will decrease (see Exhibit 8-5). The four types are:

1. Processing

2. Moving

3. Storing (waiting)

4. Inspecting

B. **Manufacturing (production) cycle time** is the time elapsed beginning with the receipt of raw materials and ending with the shipment of the final product to distributors or customers. Therefore, storage time in a finished goods warehouse is considered part of manufacturing cycle time.

C. **Manufacturing cycle efficiency (MCE),** a widely-used measure for assessing process efficiency, is the ratio of the time required by value-added activities in a value chain to the total time required by all activities in the value chain.

Manufacturing cycle efficiency =

Processing time/(Processing time + Moving time + Storing time + Inspection time).

D. Often **plant reorganization** can result in increased sales because of decreases in cycle time, and reduction in inventory-related costs because of the decrease in work-in-process inventory.

E. There are three general types of **facilities layout** that can affect cycle time of production, as well as the level of inventories and inventory-related costs.

1. **Process layout** is a means of organizing a production activity so that all similar equipment or functions are grouped together. For example, in most printing shops, similar machines are grouped together. See also the Gannett News Service example in Exhibit 8-5. Process layouts often:

    a. exist where production occurs in small batches of unique products.

    b. lead to long production paths and high work-in-process inventory levels.

2. **Product layout** is a means of organizing a production activity so that equipment or functions are organized to make a specific product. An automobile assembly line is an example of a product layout.

3. **Cellular manufacturing** is a way of organizing the plant into a number of cells so that within each cell, all machines required to manufacture a group of

similar products are arranged sequentially in close proximity to each other (see Exhibit 8-4).

Carefully work through Exhibits 8-6 through 8-10 on Glendale Electric Corporation. In Exhibit 8-10, note the cost savings from reducing the financing investment in work-in-process inventory.

Study the dialogue between Ellen Glaze (plant controller) and the production and sales managers. Interviews of this sort are extremely important to gather the necessary information to make informed decisions.

Learning Objective 5: Explain the purpose of just-in-time manufacturing systems.

IV. Just-in-Time Manufacturing

A. **Just-in-time (JIT) manufacturing** refers to making a good or providing a service only when the customer, who may be internal or external, requires it. This philosophy is based on the elimination of all nonvalue-added activities to reduce cost and time. JIT manufacturing helps avoid many of the costs and service problems associated with conventional manufacturing and facilities layout.

B. Management accounting:

1. must support the move to JIT by monitoring, identifying, and communicating to decision-makers the sources of delay, error, and waste in the system.

2. is simplified by JIT because there are fewer inventories to monitor and record.

Learning Objective 6:	Describe the cost savings resulting from reductions in inventories, reduction in production cycle time, production yield improvements, and reductions in rework and defect rates.

V. Improvements in Production Yield

The Tobor Toy Company example illustrates a company's improvements, such as decreasing rework and reducing cycle time. Thomas Archer studied the following in analyzing the situation.

A. Production flows (note the flowchart in Exhibit 8-11).

B. Work-in-process inventory.

C. Production costs (see Exhibit 8-12).

D. Cost of rework. **Rework** consists of production activities required to bring defective units up to minimum quality standards (see Exhibit 8-13).

E. Cost of carrying work-in-process inventory.

F. Incremental production costs and contribution margin per robot (see Exhibit 8-14).

G. Summary of benefits. Exhibit 8-15 summarizes the annual benefits from the Quality Improvement Program.

Work through Exhibits 8-11 to 8-15. Understanding the process that Thomas Archer went through will provide you with insight into how quality improvements can be made.

When reviewing this material, note the strong ties between management accounting and operations management. Throughout the textbook, other links related to strategy and organizational behavior are made.

PRACTICE TEST QUESTIONS AND PROBLEMS

True/False

____ 1. In general, improvements in yield rate should improve production cycle time.

____ 2. The costs and revenues that are relevant depend on the decision context and the alternatives available.

____ 3. While sunk costs are costs of resources that have been committed, they can still be influenced by the manager.

____ 4. When making a decision to purchase a new machine, the purchase price of the old machine is a relevant cost.

____ 5. When making a decision to purchase a new machine, the disposal value of an old machine is a relevant cost.

____ 6. In general, with respect to outsourcing decisions, facility-sustaining costs are avoidable costs.

____ 7. In general, outsourcing will always result in lower production costs.

____ 8. Process layouts tend to be used in organizations in which production is done in small batches.

____ 9. Production cycle time begins when raw materials are received and ends when the product is finished and sent to the finished goods warehouse.

____ 10. One of the principal inventory-related costs is that of financing the funds tied up in inventory.

Multiple-Choice

1. Each of the following should result in reductions in the level of work-in-process inventory and cycle time, EXCEPT

   (a) quality improvement programs.
   (b) corporate downsizing programs.
   (c) just-in-time programs.
   (d) cellular manufacturing.

2. Birnberg Company has collected the following information related to a decision to purchase a new machine and dispose of their old machine: The book value of the old machine is $2,000, the disposal value of the old machine is $500, the cost savings in maintenance by purchasing the new machine is $50, and the down payment on the new machine is $1,200. What is the sum of the relevant cost savings and cash inflows for the first year?

   (a) $3750
   (b) $2550
   (c) $ 550
   (d) $ 500

3. One behavioral factor that may cause managers to not replace a new machine when they should is

   (a) their reputation.
   (b) the poor salvage value of the old machine.
   (c) what to do with the old machine.
   (d) the cost of the new machine.

4. Each of the following should be considered in the make-or-buy decision, EXCEPT

   (a) unavoidable facility-sustaining costs.
   (b) the cost to produce the product
   (c) the cost to purchase the product outside the firm.
   (d) the general implications for the firm to buy the product from another firm.

5. Product layout systems store inventory primarily

   (a) at the end of the production line.
   (b) along the production line.
   (c) in large warehouses off-site.
   (d) at the beginning of the production line.

6. Each of the following kinds of costs is incurred when implementing a cellular manufacturing layout, EXCEPT

   (a) the cost of moving machines.
   (b) the cost of new insurance for workers.
   (c) the costs of training the workers.
   (d) the cost of reinstallation of the machines.

7. The financial benefits of cellular manufacturing include all of the following, EXCEPT

   (a) reduction in the number of material handlers needed.
   (b) reduction in the cost of storage.
   (c) reduction in materials wastage.
   (d) reduction in depreciation of the plant.

8. Shields Company has capacity to produce 5000 units of product HI99. Currently it is producing 3900 units. Foster Company asks Shields to produce 800 more units of HI99 for a special order. Neither new machinery nor extra plant space is needed for the special order. Which of the following statements is true?

   (a) Only product-sustaining costs will increase.
   (b) Only facility-sustaining costs will increase.
   (c) Both product-sustaining and facility-sustaining costs will increase.
   (d) Neither product-sustaining nor facility-sustaining costs will increase.

9. As the amount of work-in-process decreases, we expect all of the following to occur, EXCEPT

   (a) the wage rate per worker decreases.
   (b) inventory-related transactions decrease.
   (c) shop floor personnel decrease.
   (d) material handling decreases.

10. All of the following statements about just-in-time (JIT) are true, EXCEPT:

   (a) JIT means making a good or service only when the customer requires it.
   (b) Strictly speaking, JIT is a set of tools.
   (c) JIT production is based on the elimination of all nonvalue-added activities.
   (d) JIT is an approach to improvement that is continuous.

Completion

1. The four types of activities comprising total cycle time are: ______________, ________________, ________________, and ______________.

2. Sunk costs are not ___________ costs.

3. Cash flows at different points of time cannot be compared directly because of the _______ ________ of _________ that requires interest to be paid on bank deposits or borrowings from financial institutions.

4. ___________ means buying products from an outside supplier instead of making them in-house.

5. ____________ costs are the those eliminated when a product is discontinued.

6. Manufacturing cycle efficiency is the ratio of time required by ___________-____________ activities in a value chain to the _________ _________ required by all activities in the value chain.

7. When all machines required for the manufacture of a group of similar products are arranged sequentially in close proximity to each other, we refer to this as ____________ _____________.

8. In __________-____-________ production, no work-in-process inventories are required between the various stages of operations.

9. Two potential benefits of plant reorganization are ___________ _________ and ____________ ____________-____________ ________.

10. ___________ consists of production activities required to bring defective units up to minimum quality standards.

Problems

1. Gustafson Company is determining whether to outsource product G2A. An outside bidder has quoted a price of $52. The following costs of the product when produced in-house are shown below and expressed on a per-unit basis.

Direct materials	$13.95
Direct labor	$15.00
Unit-related overhead	$17.80
Batch-related overhead	$6.55
Product-sustaining overhead	$3.25
Facility-sustaining overhead	$8.35
	$64.90

(a) What assumptions need to be made about the behavior of support (overhead) costs?

(b) Should Gustafson Company outsource the product?

2. ALTCO purchased a stamping machine four months ago and now realizes that a much better machine is available on the market. The following information pertains to both machines.

	Old Machine	New Machine
Acquisition cost	$150,000	$200,000
Remaining life	3 years	3 years
Current disposal value	$ 60,000	--
Salvage value at the end of 3 years	$ 6,000	$ 9,000

Annual operating costs for the old machine are $60,000 and the new machine will reduce annual operating costs by $48,000. These amounts do not include any charges for depreciation. ALTCO uses the straight line method of depreciation. The estimates above also do not include rework costs. The new stamping machine also will reduce the defect rate from 4% to 2.%. All defective units are reworked at a cost of $1.25 per unit. ALTCO produces 150,000 units annually.

(a) Should ALTCO replace the old machine (ignore the time value of money)?

(b) What costs are considered sunk costs for this decision?

SOLUTIONS TO PRACTICE TEST QUESTIONS AND PROBLEMS

True/False

1. True. In general, improvements in yield rate should improve production cycle time.

2. True. The costs and revenues that are relevant depend on the decision context and the alternatives available.

3. False. Sunk costs cannot be influenced by a manager.

4. False. When making a decision to purchase a new machine, the purchase price of the old machine is a sunk cost, not a relevant cost.

5. True. When making a decision to purchase a new machine, the disposal value of an old machine is a relevant cost.

6. False. With respect to outsourcing, facility-sustaining costs (for example, those relating to building and equipment) are usually unavoidable, especially in the short run.

7. False. A general statement like this cannot be made for outsourcing. In some cases it may be less expensive to outsource and in others more expensive.

8. True. Process layouts are used for production in small batches.

9. False. Production cycle time begins with the receipt of raw materials and ends with the delivery of finished goods to distributors and customers (not to the warehouse).

10. True. Financing the funds tied up in inventory is one of the most significant inventory-related costs.

Multiple-Choice

1. b. Corporate downsizing will not result in reducing work-in-process inventory and cycle time. In fact, it might increase both if the work force is reduced significantly during downsizing.

2. c. The relevant cost savings and cash inflows are the disposal value of the old machine ($500) and the cost savings in maintenance ($50), which sum to $550.

3. a. Reputation is a critical variable for many managers. If they feel that replacing a new machine would convey that they made a mistake, they may try to save their reputation by not purchasing the new machine.

4. a. Unavoidable costs are not included in the make-or-buy decision, since they are irrelevant to the analysis.

5. b. Inventory is stored along the production line.

6. b. New insurance is not needed when cellular manufacturing is implemented.

7. d. Reduction of depreciation expense of the plant is not a financial benefit of cellular manufacturing.

8. d. Since no new machinery or floor space is needed, neither product-sustaining nor facility-sustaining costs will increase.

9. a. The wage rate per worker will not decrease.

10. b. JIT is a philosophy of manufacturing, not just a set of tools.

Completion

1. processing, moving, storing (waiting), inspecting

2. relevant

3. time value, money

4. Outsourcing

5. Avoidable

6. value added, total time

7. cellular manufacturing

8. just in time

9. increased sales [because of reduced cycle time], reduced inventory related costs

10. Rework

Problems

1. (a) Assumptions must be made about which overhead (support) costs are avoidable if Gustafson outsources the product. Batch-related and product-sustaining support costs are most likely avoidable, but facility-sustaining support costs may be unavoidable if the plant cannot be converted to another use when G2A is outsourced.

   (b) Assuming that only facility-sustaining costs are unavoidable, the relevant costs per unit of producing G2A are:

Direct materials	$13.95
Direct labor	15.00
Unit-related overhead	17.80
Batch-related overhead	6.55
Product-sustaining overhead	3.25
Total	$56.55

   The difference in cost is $56.55 - $52 = $4.55. G2A should be outsourced unless some of the other overhead costs are unavoidable and total more than $4.55.

2. (a)

Net benefits over 3 years with the new machine	New Machine - Old Machine
Salvage value difference ($9,000 - $6,000)	$ 3,000
Decrease in annual operating costs (3 years × $48,000)	144,000
Reduction in rework costs (150,000 × 2% × $1.25 × 3 years)	11,250
Acquisition of new machine	(200,000)
Current disposal value of old machine	65,000
Net cash inflow	$18,250

   Thus, ALTCO should purchase the new machine.

   (b) The acquisition cost of the old machine is a sunk cost.

Notes and Questions

Chapter 9

Budgeting: Resource Allocation to Achieve Organizational Objectives

CENTRAL FOCUS AND LEARNING OBJECTIVES

After reading this chapter, you will be able to

1. understand the primary role of budgets and budgeting in organizations.
2. describe the importance of each element of the budgeting process.
3. understand the different types of operating budgets and financial budgets and their interrelationships.
4. understand the way that organizations effectively use and interpret budgets.
5. conduct what-if and sensitivity analysis—two budgeting tools used by budget planners.
6. define the role of budgets in service and not-for-profit organizations.
7. evaluate the behavioral effects of budgeting on an organization's employees.

REVIEW OF KEY TERMS AND CONCEPTS

Learning Objective 1:	Understand the primary role of budgets and budgeting in organizations.

I. The Role of Budgets and Budgeting

A. The budgeting process determines the level of most committed costs (those that do not change with activity levels in the organization).

B. A **budget** is a quantitative model or a summary of the expected allocations to and financial consequences of the organization's short-term operating activities.

C. **Budgeting** is the process of estimating money inflows and outflows to determine a financial plan that will meet objectives.

D. Budgeting supports the management functions of planning and coordinating activities, and communicates the organization's short-term goals to its members.

E. The differences between actual results and the budget plan are called **variances.** Variances are part of a larger control system for monitoring results.

Understand the key role of budgeting, as shown in Exhibit 9-1.

Learning Objective 2:	Explain the importance of each element of the budgeting process.

Learning Objective 3:	Discuss the different types of operating budgets and financial budgets and their interrelationships.

II. The Budgeting Process

A. The **master budget** consists of operating budgets and financial budgets, usually for one year.

B. An **operating budget** is one that summarizes the financial results expected from the chosen operating plans. Firms may adapt the set of operating plans below, depending on their needs. (Box numbers below refer to Exhibit 9-2).

1. A **sales plan** (box 2) summarizes planned sales for each product.

2. A **capital spending plan** (box 3) specifies when long-term capital expenditures, such as acquisitions for buildings and special-purpose equipment must be made to meet activity objectives.

3. A **production plan** (box 5) identifies all required production.

4. A **materials purchasing plan** (box 7) schedules purchasing activities.

5. A **labor hiring and training plan** (box 8) schedules the hiring, releasing, and training of people that the organization must have to achieve its activity objectives.

6. An **administrative and discretionary spending plan** (box 9) is an operating plan that summarizes administrative and discretionary expenditures, such as advertising and research and development.

C. A **financial budget** is one that summarizes the expected financial results from the chosen operating plans. Financial budgets include:

1. a statement of projected cash flows to:

   a. plan when excess cash will be generated so that short-term investments can be made.

   b. plan how to meet any cash shortages.

2. a projected balance sheet and a projected income statement to evaluate the financial consequences of decisions; these two projected statements are generally called **pro forma** statements.

Do you understand the differences among these types of budgets? Refer to Exhibit 9-2 for the linkages among the many types of budgets.

Learning Objective 4: Understand the way that organizations effectively use and interpret budgets.

III. The Budgeting Process Illustrated: Ontario Tole Art

Carefully go through the Ontario Tole Art, Buoy Division example to understand how the budgeting process works. Work through all of the exhibits, beginning with Exhibits 9-5 and 9-6.

A. A **demand forecast** is an estimate of the sales demand at a specified selling price. The budgeting process begins with a demand forecast.

B. The sales plan is then matched with inventory policy and capacity levels and a **production plan** is determined.

C. **Aggregate planning** is an approximate determination of whether the organization has the capacity to undertake a proposed production plan.

D. **Spending plans** are developed, for example, to purchase raw materials or hire and train new employees. There are many such plans.

1. A **discretionary expenditure** is an expenditure whose short-term cost is not dictated directly by the proposed level of activities (e.g., advertising and research and development).

2. An **engineered expenditure** is one whose short-term cost is directly determined by the proposed level of activity. Engineered expenditures reflect product design and process design (e.g., materials costs and the cost of causal labor).

E. There are three major types of resources that organizations acquire that will determine their level of monthly production capacity (see Exhibit 9-7):

1. **Flexible resources** that the organization can acquire can acquire in the *short term*. Examples include many types of materials.

2. **Committed resources** that the organization must acquire for the *intermediate term*. Labor is an example.

3. **Committed resources** that the organization must acquire for the *long term*. These include plant and equipment.

F. Understanding the production plan involves the idea that production is the minimum of demand and capacity. In equation form, this is:

Production = Minimum (total demand, production capacity)

G. Financial plans including the projected balance sheet, income statement, and cash flow statement are extremely important. A **line of credit** with a financial institution is a short-term financing arrangement that allows an organization to borrow up to a prespecified limit at any time.

Continuing with the Ontario Tole Art, Buoy Division example, carefully review Exhibits 9-8 to 9-15, which include key financial statements.

Learning Objective 5: Conduct what-if and sensitivity analysis—two important budgeting tools used by budget planners.

IV. What-if Analysis

A. **What-if analysis** uses a model to predict the results of varying a model's key parameters. Through this method, a number of questions can be raised concerning specific changes to variables and their effects on the key financial indicators.

B. **Sensitivity analysis** is an analytical tool that involves selectively varying key estimates of a plan or budget. Sensitivity analysis allows planners to identify the estimates that have critical effects on decisions based on that plan. If small changes in plan parameters (estimates and relationships) produce large changes in decisions or results, the plan is said to be sensitive to the estimates.

Learning Objective 6: Define the role of budgets in service and not-for-profit organizations.

V. The Role of Budgeting in Service and Nonprofit Organizations

A. As in manufacturing organizations, budgeting helps nonmanufacturing organizations in the important functions of planning, coordination, control, and communication.

B. In the service sector, the key focus is on balancing demand for and supply of the organization's services.

C. An **appropriation** is an authorized spending limit.

See Exhibit 9-16 to see how the focus of budgeting varies in different types of organizations.

VI. Other Budgeting Concepts

A. Periodicity

1. A **periodic budget** is one that is prepared for a specified period of time, usually one year. As each budget period ends, the organization prepares a new budget for the next period.

2. **Continual budgeting** is a process that plans for a specified period of time, usually one year, and organizes a budget into budget subintervals, usually a month or a quarter. As each budget subinterval ends, the organization drops the completed subinterval from the budget and adds the next budget subinterval.

B. Controlling Discretionary Expenditures

1. **Incremental budgeting** is an approach to developing appropriations for discretionary expenditures that assumes that the starting point for each discretionary expenditure item is the amount spent on it in the previous budget.

2. **Zero-based budgeting** is an approach to developing appropriations for discretionary expenditures that assumes that the starting point for each discretionary expenditure item is zero.

3. **Project funding** is an approach to developing appropriations for discretionary expenditures that organizes appropriations into a package that focuses on achieving some defined output. For example, an organization might fund a project designed to identify and evaluate its practiced organization ethics.

Learning Objective 7: Evaluate the behavioral effects of budgeting on an organization's employees.

VII. Behavioral Aspects of Budgeting

A. Two interrelated issues are:

1. *Designing* the budget process: how the budget should be determined, who should be involved in the process, and how difficult the budget should be to attain.

a. **Authoritative budgeting** occurs when superiors simply tell subordinates what their budgets will be. Advantages include efficiency and coordination, but motivational problems among subordinates may arise.

Many organizations now have implemented **stretch targets** and use the concept of **stretch budgeting,** which means that the organization attempts to reach much higher goals with the current budget. Some believe that major innovations will occur as a result.

b. **Participative budgeting** involves a joint decision-making process in which all parties agree about setting budget targets.

c. **Consultative budgeting** occurs when managers ask subordinates to discuss their ideas but no joint decision-making occurs. This is a practical method for large organizations, but **pseudo participation** can arise if management is not sincere in its desire to incorporate subordinates' input.

2. *Influencing* the budget process: how people try to influence or manipulate the budget to their own ends.

   a. Managers play **budgeting games** in which they attempt to manipulate information and targets to achieve as high a bonus as possible.

   b. One consequence of the participation process in budgeting is that subordinates might ask for excess resources above what they need to accomplish their budget objectives. They might also understate their performance capabilities when given the opportunity so that they will be able to work under an easier budget. Both of these acts are referred to as creating **budget slack**.

PRACTICE TEST QUESTIONS AND PROBLEMS

True/False

____ 1. The master budget consists of two general types of budgets: operating budgets and financial budgets.

____ 2. The materials purchasing plan is part of the financial budget.

____ 3. The budgeting process is driven by the demand forecast.

____ 4. Asking for excess resources above what is needed to accomplish budget objectives and understating performance capabilities are both referred to as creating budget slack.

____ 5. Stretch budgeting can produce major innovations and is unlikely to have any negative repercussions.

____ 6. An engineered expenditure is one whose short-term cost is not directly determined by the proposed level of activity.

____ 7. Research shows that the most motivating types of budgets are those that are "tight" (ambitious but attainable).

____ 8. What-if analysis uses a model to predict the results of varying a model's key parameters.

____ 9. A common format used in the financing section of the cash flow statement is: Cash flow this period + Opening balance ± Changes = Closing balance.

____ 10. Zero-based budgeting and incremental budgeting are essentially the same method of budgeting.

Multiple-Choice

1. Budgeting requires the following kinds of skills, EXCEPT

   (a) experience in forecasting.
   (b) a knowledge of how activities affect costs.
   (c) the ability to see how the organization's different activities fit together.
   (d) experience in operations management.

2. Operating budgets or plans include the following, EXCEPT

(a) sales plan.
(b) capital spending plan.
(c) cash flow plan.
(d) labor hiring and training plan.

3. A demand forecast is

(a) an estimate of market demand given a product price.
(b) developed largely because of customer dissatisfaction.
(c) an estimate of market demand given the amount sold in the previous year.
(d) an estimate for the demand for labor.

4. A comparison of the production plan to productive capacity, taking into account the sales plan and inventory policy is called

(a) discretionary planning.
(b) aggregate planning.
(c) demand planning.
(d) flexible planning.

5. Which of the following is not a type of resource used to determine monthly production capacity?

(a) Flexible resources acquired for the short term
(b) Committed resources acquired for the intermediate term
(c) Fixed resources acquired for the short term
(d) Committed resources acquired for the long term

6. Committed resources are termed "committed" because:

(a) the general manager has agreed to using these resources.
(b) the resource committee of the firm has agreed to using these resources.
(c) money has been spent on the resources.
(d) the cost is the same whether the facility is used or not.

7. If forecasting errors have a critical effect on the production plan, planners say that the model is _____________ to that estimate.

   (a) related
   (b) sensitive
   (c) unrelated
   (d) insensitive

8. Each of the following is an important characteristic of a model that underlies what-if analysis, EXCEPT

   (a) the model must be complete.
   (b) the model must have been tested for at least five years.
   (c) the model must reflect relationships accurately.
   (d) the model must use reasonable estimates.

9. Incremental budgeting bases a period's expenditure level for a discretionary item

   (a) on the amount spent on that item during the previous period.
   (b) on the amount spent on that item during the previous two periods plus 15%.
   (c) at zero.
   (d) on the amount spent on that item by another division of the firm.

10. Sunset provisions are a form of ___________ _____________.

    (a) incremental budgeting.
    (b) zero-based budgeting.
    (c) project funding.
    (d) continuous budgeting.

Completion

1. The three most common methods of setting budgets are known as _________________, __________________, or ________________.

2. The ________________ method of budget setting involves a joint decision-making process in which all parties agree on the budget targets.

3. The ___________ spending plan specifies when long-term capital investments such as buildings and equipment must be made to meet activity objectives.

4. A _______________ budget is one that is prepared for a specified period of time, usually a year.

5. Paint and packing supplies are examples of __________ resources.

6. In the service sector, _________________, rather than machines, usually represent the capacity constraint, underscoring the importance of budgeting even in nonmanufacturing organizations.

7. ______ - ______ financing is usually undertaken using a line of credit established with a financial institution.

8. Planners call selectively varying a plan's or a budget's key estimates ___________ ___________.

9. Government agencies call planned cash outflows, or spending plans, ___________________.

10. The two major interrelated behavioral issues in budgeting are _______________ the budget process and _______________ the budget process.

Problems

1. Write an essay on the purpose and usefulness of budgeting.

2. Operating budgets have a number of specific types of plans associated with them. Describe each plan and its purpose.

SOLUTIONS TO PRACTICE TEST QUESTIONS AND PROBLEMS

True/False

1. True. The two general types of budgets are operating and financial budgets.

2. False. The materials purchasing plan is part of the operating budget.

3. True. The budgeting process is driven by a demand forecast.

4. True. Both these activities create budget slack.

5. False. Stretch budgeting means that the organization will try to reach much higher goals with the current budget. Although major innovations in processes, products, or services may result, workers may become frustrated or burned out, causing them to quit their jobs or simply stop trying to meet the targets.

6. False. An engineered expenditure is one whose short-term cost is directly determined by the proposed level of activity.

7. True. Standards or budgets that are too "loose" (easy to achieve) provide little motivation, but standards that are impossible to achieve can cause people, out of frustration, to stop working hard.

8. True. This is how what-if analysis is defined.

9. True. This format is a summary statement of the financing section of the cash flow statement.

10. False. Zero-based budgeting assumes the starting point for each discretionary expenditure item is zero, and incremental budgeting assumes the starting point is the amount spent on it in the previous budget.

Multiple-Choice

1. d. Operations management skill is not required for budgeting.

2. c. A cash flow plan is not included in an operating budget.

3. a. A demand forecast is an estimate of market demand given a product price.

4. b. Aggregate planning is the correct answer.

5. c. Fixed resources acquired for the short term are not a type of resource used to determine monthly production capacity.

6. d. Committed resources are termed as such because the cost is the same whether the facility is used or not.

7. b. The key idea is that the model is sensitive to that estimate.

8. b. The model does not have to be tested for five years.

9. a. Incremental budgeting bases a period's expenditure level for a discretionary item on the amount spent on that item during the previous period.

10. c. Sunset provisions are a form of project funding.

Completion

1. authoritative, participative, consultative
2. participative
3. capital
4. periodic
5. flexible
6. people
7. Short term
8. sensitivity analysis
9. appropriations
10. designing, influencing

Problems

1. Your answer should include the following elements:

   (a) Budgets are summaries of expected outcomes of an organization's short-term operating activities and are a mechanism for communicating these goals to its members.

   (b) Budgets should reflect the key features and activities of the organization and are essentially a model of how these activities are tied together in the organization.

   (c) Budgets serve a number of purposes, including organizational planning and control. Control involves coordination, identifying and solving problems, and setting a standard of performance for motivation purposes.

2. There are a number of different plans that make up an operating budget. These include:

   (a) a *sales plan* which identifies the planned level of sales for each product or service.

   (b) a *capital spending plan* which details when long-term capital investments such as plant and equipment must be made to meet objectives.

   (c) a *production plan* which identifies all required production.

   (d) a *materials purchase plan* which schedules all required purchasing activities.

   (e) a *labor hiring and training plan* which schedules the number, hiring, and training of people.

   (f) an *administrative and discretionary spending plan* which includes staffing, research and development, and advertising plans.

Notes and Questions

Chapter 10

Capital Budgeting

CENTRAL FOCUS AND LEARNING OBJECTIVES

After reading this chapter, you will be able to

1. understand the nature and importance of long-term assets.
2. discuss the basic tools and concepts of financial analysis: investment, return, future value, present value, annuities, and required rate of return.
3. understand capital budgeting as a tool to evaluate investment proposals, and the related concepts of: payback, accounting rate of return, net present value, return on investment, and economic value added.
4. explain the effect of taxes on investment decisions.
5. identify the role and nature of what-if and sensitivity analysis in capital budgeting.
6. evaluate the effects of strategic considerations on capital budgeting.
7. understand the role of post-implementation audits in capital budgeting.

REVIEW OF KEY TERMS AND CONCEPTS

Learning Objective 1: Understand the nature and importance of long-term assets.

I. The Importance of Long-Term (Capital) Assets

The focus in this chapter is on investments in long-term assets. Long-term assets create the committed costs that we have labeled batch-related, product- and process-related and facility-sustaining.

A. **Long-term or capital assets** are equipment or facilities that provide productive services to the organization for more than one year.

B. The acquisition of long-term assets is important because:

1. Organizations commit to long-term assets for extended periods of time.

2. The amount of capital committed is usually very large.

3. The long-term nature of capital assets creates technological risk for organizations.

C. **Capital budgeting** is the collection of tools that planners use to evaluate the acquisition of long-term assets based on the above considerations.

Learning Objective 2: Discuss the basic tools and concepts of financial analysis: investment, return, future value, present value, annuities, and required rate of return.

II. Basic Tools and Concepts of Financial Analysis

A. **Investment** is the monetary value of the assets that the organization gives up to acquire a long-term asset.

B. **Return** is the increased cash flows in the future as a result of the long-term asset acquired.

C. Investment and return are the foundations of capital budgeting analysis because the fundamental evaluation issue in dealing with a long-term asset is whether its future benefits justify its initial cost (the initial investment).

D. The **time value of money** is the concept that, because money can be invested to earn a return, the value of money depends on when it is received. Consequently, amounts of money received at different periods of time must be converted to their value at a common date to be compared.

E. Notation

n — **number of periods** considered in the investment analysis

FV — **future value**, or ending value, of the investment n periods from now

PV — **present value**, or value at the current moment in time, of an amount to be received n periods from now

a — **annuity**, or equal amount, received or paid at the end of each period for n periods

r — **rate of return** required, or expected, from the investment opportunity; also used to denote the rate of interest earned on an investment; sometimes called the **discount rate**

F. **Future value** is the amount to which a sum invested today will accumulate over a stated number of periods at a stated rate of interest.

1. One Period

Future value of an investment in after one year = Investment × (1 + Annual rate of interest)

$$FV = PV \times (1 + r)$$

2. Multiple Periods

a. **Compounding effect (of interest)** is the phenomenon of earning interest on interest that was previously earned over multiple periods (see Exhibit 10-3).

b. Future value of an investment in n periods = Investment × $(1 + r)^n$

$$FV = PV \times (1 + r)^n$$

c. The formula above assumes that any interest earned is not withdrawn until the end of n periods, and the annual rate of interest is constant for the n periods.

The textbook illustrates computing future values in three ways: using a calculator, a future-value table, or a computer spreadsheet program.

G. Present Value

1. **Present value** is the current monetary worth of an amount to be paid in the future under stated conditions of interest and compounding.

Present value =

$$\frac{\text{Future amount received in period n}}{(1 + \text{Required periodic return})^n}$$

$$PV = FV/(1+r)^n = FV \times (1+r)^{-n}$$

2. **Inflows** are the incremental cash inflows associated with an asset.

3. **Outflows** are the incremental cash outflows associated with an asset.

4. **Time zero (or period zero)** is the point of time when the investment is undertaken.

5. **Discounting** is the process of computing present value.

The textbook illustrates computing present values in three ways: using a calculator, a present-value table, or a computer spreadsheet program. Exhibit 10-5 illustrates the decay in present value as the interest rate increases and the time period lengthens.

H. Present Value and Future Value of Annuities

1. An **annuity** is a contract that promises to pay a fixed amount each period for a stated number of periods.

The textbook describes how to compute the present value of an annuity using a calculator, a present-value table, or a computer spreadsheet program. The formula below (see Appendix 10-1) can also be used.

2. **Present value of an annuity:**

$$PV = a \times \left[\frac{(1 + r)^n - 1}{r \times (1 + r)^n} \right]$$

3. **Annuity required to repay a loan:** Present value concepts can be applied to compute the annuity required to repay a present value. A computer spreadsheet program or the following formula (see Appendix 10-1) can be used:

$$a = PV \times \left[\frac{r \times (1 + r)^n}{(1 + r)^n - 1} \right]$$

I. Cost of Capital

1. The **cost of capital** is the minimum return that the organization must earn on its investments in order to meet its investors' return requirements.

2. The cost of capital reflects the amount and cost of debt and equity in an organization's financial structure and the financial market's perception of the financial risk of the organization's activities.

Learning Objective 3: Understand capital budgeting as a tool to evaluate investment proposals, and the related concepts of: payback, accounting rate of return, net present value, return on investment, and economic value added.

III. Alternative Approaches to Capital Budgeting

Calculations for these approaches are illustrated in the Shirley's Doughnut Hole example.

A. The **payback period** is the number of years taken for the cash inflows associated with a project to recover the initial investment. The payback period approach ignores the time value of money and ignores cash flows that occur beyond the payback period. Nevertheless, the payback period approach is widely used in practice.

B. **Accounting rate of return** is average accounting income divided by average investment (net book value). Firms may use the criterion that if the accounting rate of return for an investment is greater than a target rate of return, the investment will be undertaken. The accounting rate of return approach ignores the time value of money but considers cash flows in all periods.

C. Net Present Value

1. **Net present value** is the sum of the present values of all the cash inflows and cash outflows associated

with a project. Net present value explicitly incorporates the time value of money and considers cash flows in all periods.

2. **Period length** is the time period over which interest is computed (e.g., monthly, quarterly, semi-annually, or annually) in a capital budgeting analysis.

3. **Incremental cash flows** are cash flows that change as a result of acquiring, or disposing of, a long-term asset.

Under the net present value approach, six steps are used to determine the desirability of an investment proposal. These are: (1) Choose the period length, (2) Identify the firm's cost of capital, (3) Identify the incremental cash flows for each period, (4) Compute the present value of each period's cash flows, (5) Sum the project's present values of the cash flows to determine the project's net present value, and (6) If the net present value is positive, then the project is acceptable from an economic perspective. These steps are illustrated in the Shirley's Doughnut Hole example.

D. **Internal rate of return** is the discount rate that makes a project's net present value equal zero. Although the internal rate of return approach has distinct disadvantages, it is common in practice.

Exhibit 10-13 presents the results of a survey on organizations' investment justifications. Note that although the net present value approach is superior to the other three, all the methods are in practice.

E. **Economic value added** is the organization's income according to generally accepted accounting principles (GAAP), adjusted to reverse biases introduced by the conservative nature of GAAP, minus the organization's cost of capital multiplied by the investment in the organization. In contrast to net present value analysis, the economic value added approach begins with accounting income rather than net cash flow.

Learning Objective 4: Explain the effect of taxes on investment decisions.

IV. The Effect of Taxes on the Capital Budgeting Decision

A. The organization must pay taxes on period net benefits (taxable income).

B. Taxable income is defined by the tax jurisdiction and includes, among other things, a specification of how the organization may depreciate capital assets for tax purposes. Depreciation acts as a tax shield in that it offsets some of the taxes that would be paid. Straight-line depreciation is defined as follows:

$$\text{Depreciation} = \frac{\text{Initial Investment - Salvage Value}}{\text{Project Life}}$$

Carefully work through the capital budgeting summary example.

Learning Objective 5: Identify the role and nature of what-if and sensitivity analysis in capital budgeting.

V. **What-if analysis** and **sensitivity analysis,** discussed in Chapter 9, are especially important in capital budgeting because of their reliance on estimates of cash flows and interest rates.

Learning Objective 6: Evaluate the effects of strategic considerations on capital budgeting.

VI. Strategic benefits are important considerations in capital budgeting because they provide important competitive benefits. To be recognized in capital budgeting analysis, the benefits must be expressed in dollar terms. The key strategic benefits provided by a long-term asset are:

A. producing a product or providing a service that competitors cannot.

B. improving the quality of a product by reducing the potential to make mistakes.

C. reducing the cycle time required to make a product.

Learning Objective 7: Understand the role of post-implementation audits in capital budgeting.

VII. A **post-implementation audit** is an opportunity to reevaluate a past decision to purchase a long-lived asset by comparing expected and actual inflows and outflows. The audit provides the following benefits:

A. By comparing estimates with results, planners can determine why their estimates were incorrect and avoid making the same mistakes in the future.

B. Rewards can be given to those who make good capital budgeting decisions.

C. If the audit is not done, there are no controls on planners who might be tempted to inflate the benefits to get their projects approved.

VIII. Appendix 10-1: Annuity Formulas

A. Present Value of an Annuity

$$PV = a \times \left[\frac{(1 + r)^n - 1}{r \times (1 + r)^n} \right]$$

B. Annuity to Repay a Loan

$$a = PV \times \left[\frac{r \times (1 + r)^n}{(1 + r)^n - 1}\right]$$

IX. Appendix 10-2: Effective and Nominal Rates of Interest.

A. The **nominal rate of interest,** r_n, is the stated annual rate of interest.

B. The **effective rate of interest,** r_e, is the actual annual rate of interest earned on an investment.

$$r_e = \left(1 + \frac{r_n}{n}\right)^n - 1$$

PRACTICE TEST QUESTIONS AND PROBLEMS

True/False

____ 1. Long-term assets and capital assets refer to different concepts.

____ 2. Under the payback method, a project is accepted if its payback period is greater than a critical value.

____ 3. The time value of money applies only to investments over four years.

____ 4. *Future value* refers to the value at the current moment in time, of an amount to be received in the future.

____ 5. In conventional capital budgeting, analysts convert all cash flows to their equivalent value at time zero.

____ 6. The process of computing present value is called compounding.

____ 7. The accounting rate of return approach to capital budgeting ignores the time value of money.

____ 8. The cost of capital reflects the amount and cost of debt and equity in a firm's financial structure.

____ 9. The formula to compute future value n periods from time zero assumes that any interest earned is not withdrawn until the end of the n periods.

____ 10. Organizations can depreciate a capital investment to offset some of the taxes they would otherwise pay.

Multiple-Choice

1. All of the following are true about the payback period approach, EXCEPT that

   (a) it is widely used in practice.
   (b) it ignores cash flows that occur beyond the payback period.
   (c) it incorporates the time value of money.
   (d) it is the number of years taken for cash inflows associated with a project to recover the initial investment.

2. The future value of $1 ten years from now at an interest rate of 4% equals

   (a) $1.05.
   (b) $1.46.
   (c) $1.48.
   (d) $1.04.

3. Barney's Bread Shop has purchased equipment at a cost of $80,000. The expected life of the equipment is 5 years, and the expected salvage value at the end of 5 years is $10,000. For computing the accounting rate of return, the average investment is

   (a) $18,000.
   (b) $35,000.
   (c) $14,000.
   (d) $45,000.

4. Mitch and Doreen Shim want to accumulate $100,000 for their newborn child's education over the next 18 years. How much money at a 6% interest rate do they have to invest now to accumulate the $100,000?

   (a) $35,034.38
   (b) $ 9,235.65
   (c) $23,089.13
   (d) $37.043.15

5. The cost of capital is

(a) the maximum return an organization must earn on its investments in order to meet its investors' return requirements.
(b) the minimum return an organization must earn on its investments in order to meet its investors' return requirements.
(c) the minimum return an organization must earn on its investments that last over 5 years.
(d) the minimum return an organization must earn on its investments that last over 10 years.

6. The following are all important to calculating net present value of a new investment, EXCEPT

(a) knowing the initial purchase price of previous capital assets.
(b) determining the appropriate period length of the investment.
(c) identifying the firm's cost of capital.
(d) computing the present value of each period's cash flow.

7. Internal rate of return is

(a) the minimum return an organization must earn on its investments in order to meet its investors' return requirements.
(b) the minimum rate of return an organization chooses as its target.
(c) the actual rate of return expected from an investment.
(d) always equal to the net present value of a project.

8. Altadena Printing has just acquired a new machine for $70,000. It has a useful life of 5 years and salvage value of $7,500. If the company uses straight-line depreciation, how much depreciation can Altadena Printing claim each year?

(a) $14,000
(b) $15,500
(c) $12,500
(d) $13,000

9. Kamloops Lumber has a before-tax cash flow of $825,000 in 1996. It also has depreciation expense of $150,000 and its income is taxed at the rate of 40%. What is the after-tax cash flow for 1996?

(a) $495,000
(b) $555,000
(c) $270,000
(d) $405,000

10. Which of the following is not a benefit of performing post-implementation audits of capital budgeting decisions?

(a) Planners can identify where their estimates were incorrect.
(b) Planners will be more reluctant to inflate their estimates of benefits.
(c) Planners will be encouraged to take on more risky investments.
(d) Managers can identify and reward those who are good at making these types of decisions.

Completion

1. The long-term nature of capital assets can create ______________ and ______________________ risk for organizations.

2. ___________ __________ is the collection of tools that planners use to evaluate the acquisition of long-term assets.

3. ______________ _________ _____ ______________ is average accounting income divided by average investment.

4. _______ _____________ __________ is the sum of the present values of all the cash inflows and cash outflows associated with a project.

5. Because money has a time-dated value, a fundamental point to remember in capital budgeting is that in order to compare amounts of money received at different periods of time, the amounts must be converted to their __________ on a ___________ date.

6. An __-___________ _____________ is a contract that promises a constant amount each period over n periods.

7. ____________ ___________ __________ is an organization's GAAP income, adjusted for biases introduced by GAAP, minus the organization's cost of capital multiplied by the investment level.

8. When an amount of money is deposited in a bank and left to accumulate for multiple periods, the rate of growth is ________________.

9. What-if analysis and sensitivity analysis are important in capital budgeting because of the uncertainties in ____________ future cash flows.

10. Reviewing the decision to purchase a long-lived asset is called a ________-____________________ __________.

Problems

1. You have just found out that you won the California State Lottery. The grand prize is $18,000,000. The prize is paid out so that you will receive $360,000 every half year for the next 25 years. What is the present value of the lottery prize if the current semiannual rate of interest offered by a bank is 4%, compounded semiannually?

2. A government savings bond will pay the holder $750 in 20 years. If the bond market is now requiring 5% annual interest on government debt, what will be the present value of this bond?

3. Sarah Bonn wants to retire in 25 years with $5,000,000 in her bank. If she can invest funds to earn 12.5% compounded annually, what amount must she invest each year to accumulate $5,000,000 at the end of 25 years?

4. Bill and Shannon have decided to retire from their jobs in Ann Arbor, Michigan. Their plans are to construct an amusement park in Flint, Michigan. The amusement park building cost would be $1,000,000 per year for 2 years. The park would be open in year 3 and would generate $400,000 per year in net cash flows. Bill and Shannon have a required return of 15% on all of their investments.

   The land on which the amusement park will be built is leased, and the lease cost is included in the annual net cash flow calculation. The lease will be terminated after 10 years, and thus the park will be able to operate for 8 years. Bill and Shannon will not be compensated in any way for the work done to build the park, and will simply walk away from it when the lease is up.

   Compute the net present value of the decision to build the amusement park. Should Bill and Shannon make the investment? Ignore taxes in your analysis.

SOLUTIONS TO PRACTICE TEST QUESTIONS AND PROBLEMS

True/False

1. False. Long-term assets and capital assets refer to the same concepts.

2. False. Under the payback method, a project is accepted if its payback period is less than a critical value.

3. False. The time value of money concept can be applied for any period of time.

4. False. *Present value* refers to the value at the current moment in time, of an amount to be received in the future.

5. True. In conventional capital budgeting, analysts convert all cash flows to their equivalent value at time zero.

6. False. The process of computing present value is called discounting.

7. True. The accounting rate of return focuses on accounting income rather than on cash flows and the time value of money.

8. True. The cost of capital reflects the amount and cost of debt and equity in a firm's financial structure.

9. True. The formula also assumes the interest rate is constant for all n periods.

10. True. Organizations are allowed to depreciate a capital investment to offset some of the taxes they would otherwise pay.

Multiple-Choice

1. c. Although the payback period approach does not incorporate the time value of money or take into account cash flows beyond the payback period, it is widely used in practice.

2. c. The future value is $(1.04)^{10} = 1.48$.

3. d. The average investment is the average of the initial investment and the salvage value, or (80,000 + 10,000)/2 = $45,000.

4. a. Present value = [$100,000/(1.06)^{18}] = $35,034.38.

5. b. The cost of capital is the minimum return an organization must earn on its investments in order to meet its investors' return requirements.

6. a. Knowing the initial purchase price of previous capital assets is not necessary when calculating net present value of a new investment.

7. c. Internal rate of return is the actual rate of return expected from an investment. In other words, it is the interest rate that produces a net present value of zero for an investment.

8. c. Depreciation expense for Altadena Printing is ($70,000 - $7500)/5 = $12,500.

9. b. $825,000 - $150,000 = $675,000. $675,000 × 40% = $270,000. The after-tax cash flow is then $825,000-$270,000 = $555,000.

10. c. Under post-implementation audits, the risk and return of each investment will be evaluated, but by no means will planners always be encouraged to take on more risky projects, as a rule.

Completion

1. financial, technological
2. Capital budgeting
3. Accounting rate of return
4. Net present value
5. value, common
6. n period annuity

7. Economic value added

8. compounded (or exponential)

9. estimating

10. post implementation audit

Problems

1. Using the formula for the present value of an annuity, the prize value is \$360,000 × [$(1 + 0.04)^{50}$ -1]/[0.04 × $(1 + 0.04)^{50}$ = \$360,000 × 21.482 = \$7,733,520.

2. The present value of the bond is \$750 × [1/$(1.05)^{20}$] = \$750 × 0.377 = \$282.75.

3. This problem asks for the amount of yearly annuity payments to arrive at a *future value* of \$5,000,000. The formula for an annuity to repay a loan given a *present value* can be modified for a *future value*:

$$a = \frac{FV}{(1 + r)^n} \times \left[\frac{r \times (1 + r)^n}{(1 + r)^n - 1}\right] = FV \times \left[\frac{r}{(1 + r)^n - 1}\right]$$

   Sarah's annual payment required is therefore: \$5,000,000 × [0.125/$(1.125)^{25}$ -1] = \$5,000,000 × [0.125/18.0026] = \$34,717.

4. The incremental cost of the project is \$1,000,000 per year for 2 years. This initial investment creates an annuity of \$400,000 per year for 8 years.

   Present value of 2 years of cash outflows equals:

   \$1,000,000 × [$(1 + 0.15)^2$ - 1)/[0.15 × $(1 + 0.15)^2$] = \$1,625,708.88

   Present value of 8 years of inflows of \$400,000 (below, the present value will be adjusted for the starting point):

   \$400,000 × [$(1 + 0.15)^8$ - 1)/[0.15 × $(1 + 0.15)^8$] = \$1,794,928.60

To convert the value of the 8 years of inflows at the start of year 3, which is the same as at the end of year 2, to the present:

Present value = $1,794,928.60 × $[1/(1 + 0.15)^2]$ = $1,357,223.90

The present value of the outflows ($1,625,708.88) is greater than the present value of the inflows, $1,357,223.90. On a purely economic basis, the project should not be undertaken because its net present value is negative ($268,484.91).

Notes and Questions

Chapter 11

Planning and Control

CENTRAL FOCUS AND LEARNING OBJECTIVES

After reading this chapter, you will be able to

1. understand the organization as a nexus of contracts among stakeholder groups.
2. identify the key objectives in the organization's planning process.
3. discuss the importance and interrelationship of primary and secondary organization objectives.
4. explain the nature of the different forms of organization control
5. determine the relevance and importance of organization learning
6. explain the important role that performance measurement plays in an organization's control function.
7. understand the role of the balanced scorecard in organization control.

REVIEW OF KEY TERMS AND CONCEPTS

Learning Objective 1:	Understand the organization as a nexus of contracts among its stakeholder groups.

I. The Organization as a Nexus of Contracts

A central idea in this chapter is that an organization is a **nexus of contracts** (set of interrelated contracts) among its five stakeholder groups, who often have conflicting objectives. Contracts can be **explicit** (specifying exactly what each party contributes) or **implicit** (based on unwritten expectations). Stakeholder groups can be classified into two groups:

A. **Environment-defining stakeholders** define the organization's external environment.

1. **Owners** provide capital and are the residual claimants on the organization's assets. Owners therefore specify the organization's *primary objectives* (for example, increasing the owners' wealth).

2. **Customers** define what the organization must do to meet its primary objectives; customer requirements become part of the organization's set of *secondary objectives* (for example, providing high quality goods).

3. **The community** expects the organization to act ethically in its contracting relationships and defines the legal and moral environment in which the organization operates:

a. The organization must not violate the community's laws.

b. The organization should provide social leadership in the community.

B. **Process-defining stakeholders** work within the defined environment to design, produce, and deliver the organization's goods and services to its customers.

1. **Employees** run the organization on behalf of the owners. Because the organization's ability to meet its primary objectives depends heavily on employee

satisfaction and morale, the organization's secondary objectives should reflect employee expectations.

2. **Suppliers** are people or organizations, other than owners or employees, who provide the organization with the goods and services that it needs to design, make, sell, deliver, and maintain its products. Suppliers include creditors, who provide the organization with funds. Although, historically, tension has existed between organizations and their suppliers, some innovative organizations have turned to a more cooperative relationship with their suppliers. An organization's secondary objectives should reflect a commitment to good relationships with suppliers.

Exhibit 11-1 summarizes what the five groups of stakeholders provide to, and expect from, the organization. Why do stakeholder requirements matter?

Learning Objective 2: Identify the key activities of an organization's planning process.

II. Organization Planning

A. The organization must decide what **markets** to be in (for example, type of products to produce) and how to **compete** in those markets (for example, using a product differentiation or cost leadership strategy). This planning step defines the nature of the chosen relationship between the customer and the organization.

B. The organization must design specific **processes** (for example, manufacturing or order-taking processes) to meet its customers' requirements. This planning step defines the nature of the relationship between the organization and its employees and suppliers, and reflects community and owner requirements.

C. Organization planning effectively defines the **contracts** among the various stakeholder groups by specifying what contributions are expected from each group and what each group expects in exchange. The plan also defines what needs to be **measured.**

Learning Objective 3: Discuss the importance and interrelationship of primary and secondary organization objectives.

III. Relating Secondary and Primary Objectives

A. A **primary objective** of an organization is one specified by the organization's owners. Examples include return-on-investment targets as well as social objectives. Management must understand the causal relationship between the organization's competitive strategy and its primary objectives.

B. **Secondary objectives** are the presumed drivers, or causes, of primary objectives. The organization should define and monitor performance on a set of secondary objectives for each stakeholder group.

C. Organizations, to be successful, should evaluate their processes in terms of their intended and apparent effects on achieving the organization's primary and secondary objectives.

Exhibit 11-2 illustrates a stakeholder performance measurement system that provides a basis for learning and process improvement.

Learning Objective 4: Explain the nature of different forms of organization control.

IV. Organization Control

A. **Control** is the set of methods and tools that an organization uses to assess and improve its progress toward achieving its objectives. A system is **in control** if it is on a path leading to achieving its objectives. Otherwise, the system is **out of control**.

B. The process of keeping an organization in control requires five steps:

1. **Plan:** Develop the organization's primary and secondary objectives, and identify the processes to accomplish them.

2. **Execute:** Implement the plan.

3. **Monitor:** Measure the system's performance.

4. **Evaluate:** Identify variances between the system's objectives and actual performance.

5. **Correct:** Take corrective action to return the system to being in control.

See Exhibit 11-4 for an illustration of the cycle of control.

C. The Timing of Control

Controls can be classified by their timing relative to the controlled event.

1. **Feedback control,** also called **reactive control,** is an approach to control that reports data on completed activities to decide whether they were completed as planned or whether problems occurred.

2. **Concurrent control** is an approach to control that relies on detecting problems when they are happening so that the process can be adjusted to prevent further undesired outcomes.

3. **Feedforward control** focuses on preventing an undesired outcome before the activity is undertaken.

D. Types of Control Systems

To achieve goals, an organizational unit can be told what to do (task control) or it can be asked to use its resources and knowledge to achieve its goals (results control).

1. **Task control** (also called command and control, action control, input control, and pretransaction control) consists of systems or procedures designed to ensure that employees follow stated procedures or rules.

   a. In **preventive control**, managers design a system that can be operated only in the way that it was intended.

   b. In **audit control**, managers train employees to perform a task in a specific way and then use random audits to determine whether the employees are performing as intended.

2. **Results control** (also called decision control, outcome control, and management control) is a system focused on results or outcomes, and is designed to motivate decision-making to achieve the organization's goals.

See the two related "Consider This" examples of task and results control. Have you seen other examples?

E. Decentralization

1. **Decentralization** or employee empowerment refers to delegating decision-making responsibility.

2. Decentralization requires the support of a *results control system* that should:

   a. provide a scorecard that employees can use to evaluate needed changes and to assess their own performance.

   b. focus and motivate employee behavior.

Learning Objective 5:	Determine the relevance and importance of organization learning.

Learning Objective 6:	Explain the important role that performance measurement plays in an organization's control function.

V. Performance Measurement

The performance measurement system ties planning and control together by filling three primary roles.

A. **Focusing attention on objectives** by choosing the organization's primary and secondary objectives and choosing performance measures for these objectives.

B. **Coordination in decision-making** by providing organization members with a common set of objectives and indicating how each person contributes to those objectives. Each organization member has responsibility for managing specific secondary performance measures.

C. **Providing a basis for organization learning** by providing contemporaneous feedback on primary and secondary measures of performance. The essence of organization learning is continuously improving processes to enhance performance on secondary objectives, and continuously reevaluating and revising the causal link between secondary objectives and the organization's primary objectives. Organization learning focuses on three elements of performance.

1. How do organization processes work?

2. How do existing organization processes contribute to the organization's secondary objectives?

3. How do the organization's secondary objectives contribute to achieving its primary objectives?

☑ Exhibit 11-3 summarizes the interactions among the stakeholders, the performance measurement system, and organization learning.

Learning Objective 7: Understand the role of the balanced scorecard in organization control.

VI. The Balanced Scorecard

A. **The balanced scorecard** is a set of performance targets and an approach to performance measurement that stresses meeting all the organization's objectives relating to its primary and secondary objectives.

B. Two requirements for a balanced scorecard are:

1. **Depth:** The performance measurement system should monitor both the organization's performance and what management believes are the drivers of performance on the primary objectives.

2. **Breadth:** The performance measurement system should measure the most critical aspects or differentiators of organizational performance (those that provide unique abilities to achieve the primary objectives).

C. Implementation of a balanced scorecard requires the following:

1. Management must define the organization's primary objectives.

2. The organization must understand how stakeholders and processes contribute to its primary objectives.

3. The organization must develop a set of secondary objectives that are the drivers of performance on primary objectives.

4. The organization must develop a set of measures to monitor performance on both primary and secondary objectives.

5. The organization must develop a set of processes and implicit and explicit contracts with stakeholders to achieve the primary objectives.

6. The organization must make specific (public) statements about its beliefs concerning how processes create results.

The Bank of Montreal example illustrates implementation of a balanced scorecard. Exhibit 11-5 provides specific secondary performance measures. How would the concept of the balanced scorecard be applied to (1) a hospital emergency room, (2) a restaurant, and (3) a physician's office? Think of a variety of performance measures for each setting.

PRACTICE TEST QUESTIONS AND PROBLEMS

True/False

____ 1. Secondary objectives are the presumed drivers, or causes, of primary objectives.

____ 2. In preventive control, managers design a system that can be operated only in the way that it was intended.

____ 3. *Results control* is a system in which managers train employees to perform a task in a specific way and then use random audits to determine whether the employees are performing as intended.

____ 4. Organization learning and continuous improvement are two distinct concepts.

____ 5. Control represents the tools and methods that an organization uses to assess and improve its progress toward achieving its goals.

____ 6. Feedforward control reports data on completed activities to decide whether such activities were completed as planned.

____ 7. *Audit control* is a method or process designed to motivate compliance with stated organization goals or unit objectives.

____ 8. The terms *in control* and *out of control* apply only to manufacturing processes.

____ 9. Creditors are included in the "suppliers" stakeholder group.

____ 10. Relationships between organizations and their suppliers must inherently be adversarial.

Multiple-Choice

1. Which of the following is NOT true of an organization's stakeholder groups?

   (a) They have been described as a nexus of contracts.
   (b) They all specify the organization's primary objectives.
   (c) They can be subject to both explicit and implicit contracts.
   (d) They sometimes have conflicting objectives.

2. All of the following are common steps in the planning and control process, EXCEPT

   (a) setting objectives.
   (b) measuring performance.
   (c) comparing performance to goals.
   (d) analyzing variances only if they are greater than 10%.

3. Feedforward control

   (a) happens before the good or service is delivered.
   (b) happens when a good or service is being made.
   (c) happens when a good or service has been completed or delivered.
   (d) happens in the following performance period.

4. In which of the following situations would task control be least useful?

   (a) Operating nuclear-generating facilities
   (b) Handling large amounts of cash
   (c) Preparing food in a fast-food restaurant
   (d) A rapidly changing environment

5. All of the following are benefits of delegated decision-making responsibility, EXCEPT that people on the "front lines"

   (a) are motivated to make decisions that will benefit the organization.
   (b) should be the first to see any need for change.
   (c) can respond most quickly to a need for change.
   (d) are in the best position to develop the knowledge required to understand needed changes in their own jobs.

6. All of the following are true about performance measurement, EXCEPT:

   (a) It supports organization learning.
   (b) It helps coordinate individual decision-making.
   (c) It involves choosing the performance measures for the organization's primary and secondary objectives.
   (d) It has little to do with planning.

7. To provide a balanced scorecard, a performance measurement system should do all of the following, EXCEPT

   (a) monitor the causes of performance on the primary objectives.
   (b) provide information for external financial reporting.
   (c) monitor the causes of performance on the primary objectives.
   (d) provide understanding of how processes create results.

8. A SWOT analysis includes all of the following with respect to an organization, EXCEPT

   (a) strengths.
   (b) weaknesses.
   (c) opportunities.
   (d) time value of money.

9. Which of the following is least important for management?

   (a) Understanding the causal relationship between the organization's competitive strategy and its primary objectives.
   (b) Understanding the causal relationship between the organization's primary and secondary objectives and measures.
   (c) The input-output relationship with the organization's stakeholders.
   (d) Holding organization members accountable only for the results they create.

10. Organization planning involves all of the following, EXCEPT

(a) taking corrective action to return a system to being in control.
(b) deciding what markets to be in.
(c) deciding how to compete in the chosen markets.
(d) defining what should be measured.

Completion

1. Environment-defining stakeholders include the ______________, ______________, and ______________.

2. Process-defining stakeholders include ______________ and ______________.

3. ______________ ______________ is an approach to control that reports data on completed activities to decide whether they were completed as planned or whether problems occurred.

4. The ______________ ______________ is a set of performance targets and results that reflect the organization's performance in meeting its objectives relating to its customers, employees, business partners, shareholders, and community.

5. Once the organization has identified which stakeholders it intends to serve and the level of its commitments to each stakeholder group, its expresses this commitment in its ______________ ______________

6. ______________ control happens while the good or service is being produced and is used to detect unfavorable outcomes and correct the process.

7. A method or a process designed to enforce compliance with stated organization rules is called a ______________ ______________ method or process.

8. Decentralization requires the support of a ______________ control system.

9. Rather than maximizing wealth, for-profit organizations more likely engage in a process of Satisfizing. That is, they aim to achieve a return on investment for owners that meets or exceeds the owners' expectations, given the risk of the investment.

10. Among the five stakeholder groups, Customers define what the organization must do to meet the organization's primary objectives

Problems

1. Why are control systems necessary for organizations?

2. What are some likely factors that customers will use to evaluate a restaurant? Provide specific ways in which the restaurant owners might evaluate performance on these factors.

SOLUTIONS TO PRACTICE TEST QUESTIONS AND PROBLEMS

True/False

1. True. Achieving secondary objectives is the means to achieving primary objectives.

2. True. In preventive control, which is a form of task control, managers design a system that can be operated only in the way that it was intended.

3. False. *Audit control* is a system in which managers train employees to perform a task in a specific way and then use random audits to determine whether the employees are performing as intended.

4. False. Continuous improvement is a fundamental aspect of organization learning.

5. True. Control represents the tools and methods that an organization uses to assess and improve its progress toward achieving its goals.

6. False. *Feedback* control reports data on completed activities to decide whether such activities were completed as planned.

7. False. *Results control* is a method or process designed to motivate compliance with stated organization goals or unit objectives.

8. False. These terms describe whether a system is on a path leading to an organization's or unit's objectives, and hence apply to manufacturing and nonmanufacturing settings.

9. True. Creditors "supply" the organization with funds.

10. False. Innovative organizations have discovered that cooperation and long-term relationships with suppliers can increase profitability for both parties.

Multiple-Choice

1. b. Owners specify the primary objectives of an organization.

2. d. Analyzing variances only if they are greater than 10% is an arbitrary rule.

3. a. Feedforward control happens before the good or service is delivered.

4. d. Task control, which is the process of ensuring that a task is completed in a predetermined manner, is difficult to achieve in an environment that is rapidly changing.

5. a. Although delegated decision-making provides many benefits, it requires the support of a results control system that helps provide motivation for employees to meet the organization's objectives.

6. d. Performance measurement provides a critical link between planning and control.

7. b. The balanced scorecard is designed for internal management use.

8. d. The correct answer is "threats."

9. d. Focusing only on results that members are accountable for is detrimental to viewing the organization as a chain of processes with a common objective.

10. a. Taking corrective action to return a system to being in control is a control function.

Completion

1. community, owners, customers
2. employees, suppliers
3. Feedback control (or reactive control)
4. balanced scorecard
5. mission statement
6. Concurrent
7. task control

8. results

9. satisficing

10. customers

Problems

1. Control systems serve a very important purpose in organizations. First, the planning function is quite meaningless without control. Control systems provide tools and methods that organizations use to assess and improve their progress towards achieving goals that are specified by the planning function. Generally, five steps are involved. First, goals are set and the processes to accomplish the goals are identified. Second, the plan is implemented. Third, the system's performance is measured, and fourth, variances (comparisons between performance and goals variances) are analyzed. Finally, any necessary corrective action is taken. The control system then cycles through the process again.

   There are many types of control systems, including feedforward control, concurrent control, and feedback control. All three provide different types of information about an organization's processes. Feedforward and concurrent control are very effective at correcting problems either before they occur or as they are occurring. Relatively speaking, feedback control is weak, as the information that is generated is usually well after an event has occurred.

2. Some factors that customers are likely to use to evaluate a restaurant include: (a) cost of a meal, (b) quality of food, (c) quality of service, and (d) general atmosphere.

   Specific ways in which the restaurant owners might evaluate performance on these factors include: (a) comparing costs to those of competitors, (b) recording the number of compliments and complaints by customers and food experts (such as writers in local papers and magazines), (c) recording the number of compliments and number of complaints about the attitudes and behavior of servers and other employees, and timeliness of food delivery, and (d) recording the number of compliments and number of complaints about the restaurant's atmosphere. A key overall measure of performance is the number of repeat customers.

Notes and Questions

Chapter 12

Financial Control

CENTRAL FOCUS AND LEARNING OBJECTIVES

After reading this chapter, you will be able to

1. discuss the design and use of responsibility centers in an organization.
2. understand the issues to consider and basic tools to use in assessing the performance of a responsibility center.
3. recognize the common forms of responsibility centers.
4. evaluate the issues and problems created by revenue and cost interactions in evaluating the performance of an organization unit.
5. discuss transfer-pricing alternatives in organizations.
6. understand the use of return on investment and economic value added as financial control tools.
7. identify the limitations of using financial controls.

REVIEW OF KEY TERMS AND CONCEPTS

I. The Role and Contribution of Financial Control

This chapter discusses issues relating to using financial information in the process of organization control.

Learning Objective 1: Discuss the design and use of responsibility centers in an organization.

II. Decentralization

A. **Centralization** occurs when decision-making is reserved for senior managers. Typically centralization works effectively in organizations that face stable environments and technologies, and where customer requirements are well understood.

B. **Decentralization** is the strategy of delegating decision-making responsibility from senior management to employees at lower levels of the organization. Decentralization is effective in organizations whose:

1. environments, technologies, and customer requirements are constantly changing.

2. employees have the skills and knowledge to accept decision-making responsibility.

3. employees understand the organization's objectives so that they can make decisions that are consistent with those objectives.

Learning Objective 2: Understand the issues to consider and basic tools to use in assessing the performance of a responsibility center.

III. Basic Issues and Tools

A. **Operations control** views control from the point of view of process improvements.

B. **Financial control** is the formal evaluation of some financial facet of an organization or a responsibility center. Common financial measures include revenue, cost, profit, return on investment, and economic value added. Financial control helps identify the poorly performing areas of an organization and suggests where improvements can be made.

C. A **responsibility center is** an organizational subunit for which a manager has been assigned accountability.

Learning Objective 3: Recognize the common forms of responsibility centers.

D. A **cost center** is a responsibility center whose employees control costs but do not control its revenues or investment level.

1. Comparing Budgeted and Actual Results

When budgeted and actual results are compared, variances can arise. When actual costs are greater than budgeted costs, an unfavorable variance occurs (see Chapter 5), but when the budgeted costs are greater than actual costs, a favorable variance exists.

See Exhibits 12-1, 12-2, and 12-3 for simple variance analyses. Note, in particular, that Exhibit 12-3 illustrates an inappropriate comparison (variance analysis) between actual costs for one set of production levels, and budgeted costs for a different set of production levels. The flexible budget concept provides a more appropriate variance analysis.

2. The Flexible Budget

The key concept in flexible budgeting is that cost targets in the planned or master budget are recast to reflect the actual level of production. This allows comparisons of costs by holding volume constant. Without holding volume constant, a manager is comparing "apples to oranges," (costs at differing volume levels), rather than "apples to apples," (costs at the same volume levels).

Study Exhibits 12-4 and 12-5 to understand the "apples to apples" comparison.

E. A **revenue center** is a responsibility center whose employees control revenues but do not control manufacturing or acquisition costs of the products or services they sell, or the level of investment. Revenue center employees can control the mix of items carried in their stores, prices of products, and promotional activities. Revenue center managers are often at the mercy of others who determine the costs of their goods (e.g., service station managers have no control over the cost of the gas they sell). Focusing only on revenues may cause managers to increase the use of activities that create costs in order to promote higher revenue levels.

F. A **profit center** is a responsibility center whose employees control revenues and costs but not the level of investment. The level of investment is usually controlled by senior management. Many outlets of fast-food restaurant chains are profit centers.

G. An **investment center** is a responsibility center whose employees control its revenues, costs, and the level of investment. The investment center is essentially an independent business.

Exhibit 12-6 summarizes the differences among the various types of responsibility centers.

Learning Objective 4: Evaluate the issues and problems created by revenue and cost interactions in evaluating the performance of an organization unit.

IV. Evaluating Responsibility Centers

A. **Controllability,** a principle often used in control, asserts that people should be held accountable only for results that they can control. The main application of this principle is that managers should not be held accountable for revenues, costs, or investments outside their control. One major difficulty in applying this occurs when revenues and costs are jointly earned or incurred. Separating these component revenues and costs can involve intricate, and sometimes arbitrary, accounting procedures.

B. A **segment margin** is the level of controllable profit reported by an organizational unit or product line. Each unit's segment margin is an estimate of its short-term effect on the organization's profit.

Interpreting segment margins should be done carefully, as:

1. Segment margins can represent highly aggregated summaries of each organizational unit's performance. Other critical success factors should be used as well to assess performance.

2. Some segment reports contain arbitrary numbers. Accountants call these **soft numbers** because they rest on subjective assumptions over which there can be legitimate disagreement.

3. The revenue figures often reflect assumptions and allocations that can be misleading. These assumptions relate to the transfer-pricing issue–how the revenues that the organization earned are divided among the responsibility centers.

Study Exhibit 12-7 on segment reporting at Earl's Motors. Note the breakdown of costs to arrive at the segment margin.

Learning Objective 5: Discuss transfer-pricing alternatives in organizations.

V. Transfer Pricing

A. **Transfer pricing** is a set of tools and methods used to attribute revenues earned by the organization to organization subunits. *Transfer pricing can be very arbitrary, especially if there is a high degree of interaction among the various responsibility centers.*

There are four major approaches to transfer pricing:

1. Market-Based Transfer Prices

Market prices provide an independent valuation of products that are transferred between divisions and reflect jointly-earned revenue in a manner that reflects the market's assessment. One difficulty is that clear market prices often do not exist for many products.

2. Cost-Based Transfer Prices

If goods or services do not have clear market prices, transfer prices are often based on cost. Common cost-basis methods include variable cost plus a markup, full cost, and full cost plus a markup.

Some concerns about cost-based transfer prices are:

a. Economists argue that only marginal-cost transfer prices are optimal and that any other method results in economic losses for the overall organization.

b. Cost-based transfer does not focus on the intent of the transfer-pricing system, which is to allow computation of unit incomes.

c. Cost-based transfer does not provide incentives to the supplying division to control costs, because the supplier can always recover its costs.

d. Cost-based transfers do not provide the appropriate economic guidance when operations are capacity-constrained.

3. Negotiated Transfer Prices

When market prices do not exist, another possibility is to allow divisions to negotiate transfer prices. Critics argue that these types of prices reflect both negotiating skills and economic considerations, not just economics alone.

In an economic sense, the optimal transfer price occurs when the purchasing division offers to pay the supplying division the **net realizable value** of the last unit supplied for all of the units supplied. The net realizable value is the difference between a product's revenue and the additional costs needed to put the product in the customer's hands. See Appendix 12-1 for a mathematical treatment of the optimal quantity to transfer.

4. Administered Transfer Prices

Administered transfer prices are set by an arbitrator or by a rule or policy. Some find them appealing because they are easy to administer. An example is to use the variable cost of a product plus 25%. Others view these types of prices as unappealing because they are quite arbitrary. Administrative transfer prices are usually based on cost, but may also be based on equity considerations designed around some definition of a reasonable division of a jointly-earned revenue or a jointly-incurred cost.

Review Exhibit 12-12, which summarizes the above four major transfer-pricing approaches. Do you understand the differences among these methods?

B. Cost Allocations to Support Financial Control

Even with all of the problems with evaluating responsibility center income statements, many organizations do produce the statements. Each must be studied carefully and with a critical eye. One of the key issues involves allocating jointly-incurred costs. Finding the most appropriate cost driver requires careful analysis, as we have been stressing throughout the text.

See Exhibits 12-10 and 12-11 on Shirley's Grill and Bar to see how indirect costs are allocated based on different allocation bases.

C. Assigning and Valuing Assets in Investment Centers

Other problems associated with evaluating investment centers relate to how to assign responsibility for jointly used assets, such as cash and plant and equipment, and for jointly created assets, such as accounts receivable. Once these assets are assigned to investment centers, a method of costing, such as historical cost or replacement cost, must be chosen.

Learning Objective 6: Understand the use of return on investment and economic value added as financial control tools.

VI. Return on Investment and Economic Value Added

A. Efficiency and Productivity Elements of Return on Investment

In Chapter 1, we discussed Dupont's development of the return-on-investment (ROI) concept. The ROI concept is:

$$\text{ROI} = \text{Operating Income/Investment}$$

$$= \frac{\text{Operating Income}}{\text{Sales}} \times \frac{\text{Sales}}{\text{Investment}}$$

$$= \text{Return on sales} \times \text{Asset turnover}$$

$$= \text{Efficiency} \times \text{Productivity}$$

1. **Efficiency** is a measure of an organization's ability to control costs. As shown above, in financial control, this is the ratio of earnings to sales (also called return on sales or sales margin).

2. **Productivity** is a ratio of output to input. In financial control, as shown above, this is the ratio of sales to investment.

Exhibit 12-13 details the Dupont ROI Control System.

B. Assessing Return on Investment: Ratio Trends

1. Define what is meant by investment. A possibility is total assets minus accumulated depreciation.

2. Compute ROI and decompose ROI into its efficiency and productivity measures. These measures, as well as total ROI, are most useful when evaluating trends over time and when comparing the numbers with those of the best competitor.

   a. Trend analysis compares sequential measures for the same organization.

   b. Cross-sectional analysis compares the same measure for different organizations during the same time period.

3. This type of analysis can be very useful, but it is only a first step. *Ratio analysis does not identify a problem or a solution. Rather, it points to where analysis can begin.*

4. ROI should be viewed as a method to evaluate the desirability of long-term investments, rather than as a way to measure short-term performance of a manager. Organizations should ROI measures so that a manager's decisions reflect the organization's goals. A particularly undesirable situation arises when the manager is told to make return on investment as large as possible or to increase average return on investment to a target level. In this case, the manager may inappropriately turn down projects whose internal rate of return exceeds the organization's cost of capital.

Study Exhibits 12-14 through 12-18 on Dorchester Manufacturing for an illustration of the use of ratio trends.

C. Economic Value Added

1. **Economic value added** analysis (a form of residual income), also called **economic value analysis** or **shareholder value analysis**, evaluates an organization segment's (for example, a division's, product line's, or product's) financial desirability using the segment's income, less a financial charge that is computed by multiplying the organization's cost of capital by the investment in the segment. The income amount and the investment amount used in economic value added analysis is GAAP income adjusted to reverse the conservative bias introduced by GAAP. For example, GAAP requires the immediate expensing of research and development costs, but in computing economic value added, research and development costs are capitalized and expensed over a period of years.

2. Economic value added is used primarily to encourage managers to improve the relationship between return and assets employed. Managers can, for example, make assets more efficient or use assets more effectively.

3. Unlike with ROI, a manager attempting to maximize economic value added should undertake investments that are expected to earn more than their cost of capital.

Learning Objective 7: Identify the limitations of using financial controls.

VII. The Efficacy of Financial Control

Financial control has been criticized for three reasons:

A. Measures of financial control are too narrow and do not measure other important performance variables, such as product or service quality, and customer service.

B. Financial measures of control focus on aggregate results rather than the manageable causes of those results.

C. Many times, financial control is too focused on short-term results. This is not a problem inherent to financial control. Rather it is a problem relating to how financial control can be misused. A short-term focus can be debilitating for all employees, especially because this kind of an orientation produces behaviors that are not in the best long-run interests of the organization.

PRACTICE TEST QUESTIONS AND PROBLEMS

True/False

____ 1. Centralization is more suited (than is decentralization) to entities whose environments are stable.

____ 2. To assess variances accurately when actual volume differs from planned volume, flexible budgets should be used.

____ 3. Investment centers are a combination of profit and cost centers.

____ 4. The controllability principle applies only to managers of cost centers.

____ 5. If Division A supplies goods to Division B, and both divisions are investment centers, the transfer price will affect the incomes of both divisions.

____ 6. When a good or service has no market price, one alternative is to consider using cost as a transfer price.

____ 7. Cost-based transfer pricing provides incentives to the supplying division to control costs.

____ 8. Another way to state ROI is: Efficiency $\times$ Productivity.

____ 9. ROI measures are most useful when evaluating trends over time and when comparing the numbers with those of the best competitor.

____ 10. *Economic value added* is a variation of the ROI formula.

Multiple-Choice

1. Each of the following is true about centralization, EXCEPT:

   (a) Centralization is more suited to organizations in stable environments.
   (b) Under centralization, technology and customer requirements are well understood.
   (c) Under centralization, product lines are mostly of the commodity type.
   (d) Under centralization, employee empowerment programs are firmly in place.

2. Investment center managers are responsible for

   (a) costs and investments.
   (b) revenues.
   (c) revenues and investments.
   (d) costs, revenues, and investments.

3. Segment margin reports should be interpreted carefully because

   (a) the segment margin may contain numbers that are quite arbitrary.
   (b) segment margins do not take variable costs into account.
   (c) segment margins do not take fixed costs into account.
   (d) segment margins are never calculated by product line.

4. Which of the following transfer-pricing methods are set by the application of a rule or policy?

   (a) Market-based transfer price
   (b) Administered transfer price
   (c) Cost-based transfer price
   (d) Negotiated transfer price

5. The biggest problem with market-based transfer prices is that

   (a) they do not allow both parties to calculate unit incomes.
   (b) they require too much negotiation.
   (c) market prices seldom exist.
   (d) they do not provide the proper economic guidance.

6. Return on investment is the ratio of

(a) operating income to productivity.
(b) efficiency to investment.
(c) operating income to investment.
(d) operating income to sales.

7. If ROI = 20%, the sales level is $1,000,000, and the investment level is $1,500,000, what is the operating income?

(a) $7,500,000
(b) $5,000,000
(c) $ 300,000
(d) $ 200,000

8. If, for purposes of computing economic value added, accounting income is 12% of sales, $3,000,000 of capital is used, the cost of capital is 9%, and sales is revenue is $15,000,000, what is the economic value added?

(a) $1,530,000
(b) $ 990,000
(c) $ 900,000
(d) $ 450,000

9. All of the following are true about cost center control, EXCEPT:

(a) Cost centers should be evaluated solely on their ability to control costs.
(b) Interperiod cost comparisons can be misleading when the production mix or the production levels are changing.
(c) Flexible budgets should be used to compute variances from actual results.
(d) Positive variances are labeled "unfavorable."

10. Financial control is thought by some to be an ineffective method of control for all of the reasons below, EXCEPT:

(a) Financial control often ignores nonquantitative factors such as quality and customer satisfaction.
(b) Financial control measures the overall effect of performance on critical success factors, but does not provide direct insight on individual critical success factors.
(c) Financial control is often oriented toward short-term performance.
(d) Financial control does not provide an overall assessment of whether the organization's strategies and decisions are providing acceptable financial returns.

Completion

1. ________________ allows organization members to identify changing customer tastes quickly and gives employees authority and responsibility.

2. ______________ control focuses on finding the best operating decisions; ______________ control focuses on an overall assessment of how well systems are working to create financial results.

3. Cost centers are ___________________ centers whose employees control costs but do not control their _____________ or ________________ level.

4. Some ______________ centers control the mix of stock carried, price, and promotional activities.

5. A ___________ center is like an independent business except senior management controls the level of investment.

6. A ______________ ____________ is the level of controllable profit reported by an organization unit or product line.

7. Numbers that can be quite arbitrary because they rest on subjective assumptions over which there can be legitimate disagreement are called _________ numbers.

8. If an organization is committed to the spirit of determining the income of each responsibility center, ____________ ____________ are the most appropriate basis for transferring goods or services between responsibility centers.

9. Some theoreticians object to ________________ ____________ ____________ because the resulting profits of the responsibility centers reflect both economic considerations and negotiating skills, rather than purely economic considerations.

10. Return on investment = return on sales × ________ ____________.

Problems

1. You have just purchased a fast food franchise called Mr. Chicken. World-wide there are 700 such franchises. Do you think that your franchise can be run as an investment center?

2. Compare and contrast the four major methods of transfer prices: market-based transfer prices, cost-based transfer prices, negotiated transfer prices, and administered transfer prices.

SOLUTIONS TO PRACTICE TEST QUESTIONS AND PROBLEMS

True/False

1. True. Centralization is more suited to entities whose environments are stable.

2. True. Flexible budgets should be used when actual volume differs from planned volume.

3. False. Investment centers are responsibility centers whose managers control revenues, costs, and the level of investment.

4. False. The controllability principle applies to managers of all types of responsibility centers.

5. True. The transfer price represents sales revenue for Division A, and cost for Division B.

6. True. When a good or service has no market price, one alternative is to consider using cost as a transfer price.

7. False. Cost-based transfer pricing does *not* provide incentives to the supplying division to control costs, because the supplier can always recover its costs.

8. True. Another way to state ROI is: Efficiency × Productivity, where Efficiency = Return on sales, and Productivity = Asset turnover.

9. True. Total ROI, as well as its associated submeasures, can be tracked using trend analysis or cross-sectional analysis

10. False. Economic value added relies on the residual income concept. That is, economic value added is a segment's income, minus the cost of capital multiplied by the investment in the segment.

Multiple-Choice

1. d. In most centralized firms, decision-making is centralized and employee empowerment programs are not overly abundant.

2. d. Investment center managers are responsible for costs, revenues, and investments.

3. a. Segment margins should be interpreted because they may contain numbers that are quite arbitrary.

4. b. Administered transfer prices are set by the application of a rule or policy.

5. c. The biggest problem with market-based transfer prices is that market prices seldom exist.

6. c. Return on investment is the ratio of operating income to investment.

7. c. ROI = Operating income/Investment; 0.20 = Operating income/$1,500,000, so Operating income = $300,000. The sales level is unnecessary in this solving this problem.

8. a. Economic value added = accounting income - cost of capital times investment; 12% ($15,000,000) - 9% ($3,000,000) = $1,530,000.

9. a. Cost centers should be also be evaluated on quality and other critical nonfinancial indicators.

10. d. Financial control does provide an overall assessment of whether the organization's strategies and decisions are providing acceptable financial returns.

Completion

1. Decentralization
2. Operations, financial
3. responsibility, revenues, investment
4. revenue
5. profit
6. segment margin

7. soft

8. market prices

9. negotiated transfer prices

10. asset turnover

Problems

1. As manager of Mr. Chicken, you will probably have very little control over the food that you will be serving, prices that you can charge, and the kind of advertising that you can use. This is because many of these decisions will be made at the corporate level. However, as manager, you can control the level and quality of customer service, personnel, and cleanliness. These are critical variables to maximize return business. In addition, the major aspects of an investment center, such as building costs and inventory, are not controllable by the manager. Thus, it is more appropriate to operate this type of business as a profit center.

2. Market-based prices have the advantage of being objective and provide the appropriate economic incentives as long as a market price exists. A key disadvantage is that no market prices may be available for the exact product transferred. Cost-based prices are relatively easy to use, as the data are usually available from the cost accounting system. There are many transfer price variations associated with costs; any variation other than marginal cost will not provide the right economic incentives. Negotiated transfer prices do reflect the concept of responsibility, but since negotiating skill is a critical factor in determining prices, critics charge that such prices do not reflect enough of the economics of the situation. Finally, administered transfer prices are simple to administer, as they are based on established rules. However, administratively set prices violate the spirit that underlies the responsibility philosophy.

Notes and Questions

Chapter 13

Contemporary Management Accounting: Methods to Stay Competitive

CENTRAL FOCUS AND LEARNING OBJECTIVES

After reading this chapter, you will be able to

1. describe the total life cycle costing approach to managing product costs in a comprehensive manner.
2. explain the method of target costing—a management accounting method used to reduce product costs before the manufacturing cycle begins.
3. understand the importance and use of Kaizen costing—a method used to reduce process costs during the manufacturing cycle.
4. understand the importance and process of controlling the costs of nonconformance of products to established quality standards.
5. understand a model for benchmarking the best practices of other organizations.
6. show how to apply the benchmarking model to learning about advances in management accounting methods.

REVIEW OF KEY TERMS AND CONCEPTS

I. Introduction and Organizing Framework

A. This chapter focuses on innovations in management accounting methods developed to evaluate the performance of product design and development activities.

B. The methods covered include the total life cycle product costing approach, target costing, Kaizen costing, cost of nonconformance (CONC), and benchmarking.

Note Exhibit 13-1, which illustrates the relationships among life cycle concepts and new management accounting methods.

Learning Objective 1: Describe the total life cycle costing approach to managing product costs in a comprehensive manner.

II. Total Life Cycle Product Costing: A Comprehensive Approach to Cost Management

This approach, which is sometimes called whole life product costing, integrates three life cycle concepts:

A. The Research, Development, and Engineering (RD&E) Cycle.

This cycle has three stages:

1. Market research to assess emerging customer needs, leading to idea generation for new products.

2. Product design (development of technical aspects of the product).

3. Product development (incorporation of critical features and design of prototypes, production processes, and special tooling).

Exhibit 13-2 shows the relationship between costs committed and costs incurred. Note that a dollar spent on activities in this stage can save $8 to $10 on manufacturing and post-manufacturing activities, such as design changes or service costs.

B. The Manufacturing Cycle

1. During this stage, there is often little room for engineering flexibility to influence product costs and product design, as these have been set in the previous cycle.

2. As noted in Chapter 8, operations management decisions, such as the implementation of JIT, can help to reduce manufacturing life cycle costs.

C. The Post-Sale Service and Disposal Cycle

1. This cycle begins once the first unit of product is in the hands of the customer. Thus, there is overlap with the manufacturing cycle.

2. This cycle has three stages:

   a. Rapid growth, from the first shipment through the growth stage of the product's sales cycle.

   b. Transition, from the peak of the sales cycle to the peak in the service cycle.

   c. Maturity, from the peak in the service cycle to the time of the last shipment made to a customer.

Exhibit 13-3 provides a breakdown of life cycle costs across four types of products.

Learning Objective 2: Explain the method of target costing—a management accounting method used to reduce product costs before the manufacturing cycle begins.

III. Target Costing

A. Target costing is a method of cost planning focused on reducing costs for products that require discrete manufacturing processes and reasonably short product life cycles.

B. Target costing is used during the RD &E cycle.

See Exhibit 13-4 for a comparison of traditional cost reduction versus Japanese target costing, and Exhibit 13-5 for a target-costing example.

C. **Traditional cost reduction** begins with market research into customer requirements, followed by product specification. Traditionally, at this stage, product cost is not a significant factor for product design. After the engineers and designers have determined product design, they estimate product cost (C_t), where the *t* subscript indicates numbers derived under traditional thinking. If the estimated cost is considered too high, then it might be necessary to modify product design. In order to find the desired profit margin (P_t) it is necessary to subtract the estimated cost from the expected selling price (S_t). The profit margin is the result of the difference between the expected selling price and the estimated production cost. This relationship in the traditional system is expressed below with the following equation:

$$P_t = S_t - C_t$$

D. Under the **cost-plus method**, an expected profit margin (P_{cp}) is added to the expected product cost (C_{cp}), where the subscript *cp* indicates numbers derived under cost-plus thinking. Selling price (S_{cp}), then, is simply the result of the sum of these two variables. In equation form, this relationship for the cost-plus approach is expressed as:

$$S_{cp} = C_{cp} + P_{cp}$$

As in the traditional method described above, product designers do not attempt to achieve a particular cost target.

E. Under **target costing**, both the sequence of steps and way of thinking about determining product costs differ significantly from traditional costing (see Column 2, Exhibit 13-4). The first two steps, market research to determine customer requirements and product specification, are similar to traditional costing. After these initial steps, the process is quite different. The next step, determining a **target selling price (S_{tc})** and **target product volume**, depends on the company's perceived value of the product to the customer. The subscript *tc* indicates numbers derived under the target-costing approach The **target profit margin (P_{tc})** results from a long-run profit analysis, often based on return on sales (net income/sales). The **target cost (C_{tc})** is the difference between the target selling price and the target profit margin.. This relationship for the target-costing approach is shown in the following equation:

$$C_{tc} = S_{tc} - P_{tc}$$

Once the target cost is set, the company must determine target costs for each component.

F. The **value engineering** process examines each component of a product to determine whether it is possible to reduce costs while maintaining functionality and performance. Several iterations of value engineering usually are required before it is possible to determine the final target cost.

G. Concerns about target costing include:

1. Conflicts can arise among parties (e.g., manufacturing and marketing) if the entire organization does not understand and commit to the target-costing process.

2. Under target costing, employees, especially design engineers, experience a great amount of pressure to meet goals, leading to burnout.

3. Development time may increase as a result of repeated value engineering cycles to reduce costs. This may slow time to market.

Learning Objective 3: Understand the importance and use of Kaizen costing—a method used to reduce process costs during the manufacturing cycle.

IV. Kaizen costing

A. **Kaizen costing** is similar to target costing in its cost reduction mission, except that it focuses on the manufacturing stage of the total life cycle.

B. Kaizen means making improvements to a process through small, incremental amounts, rather than through large innovations.

C. There are fewer opportunities to effect major changes with Kaizen costing than with target costing because Kaizen costing occurs once the product and manufacturing process have been designed.

Exhibit 13-6 illustrates one approach to computing Kaizen costs for plants, and Exhibit 13-7 compares standard costing to Kaizen costing.

D. **Kaizen costing** differs from **standard costing** in the following ways:

1. Under standard costing, a cost control system concept is used, stability in current manufacturing processes is assumed, and the goal is to meet performance standards. However, under Kaizen costing, a cost reduction concept is used, continuous improvement in manufacturing is assumed, and the goal is to achieve cost reduction standards.

2. Under standard costing, standards are set annually or semiannually, cost variance analysis involves comparing actual to standard costs, and cost variance investigation occurs when standards are not

met. Under target costing, cost reduction targets are set and applied monthly, and Kaizen methods are applied all year long to achieve targets.

3. Managers and engineers are assumed to have the best knowledge to reduce costs under standard costing, while workers who are closest to the process are thought to have the best insight into how cost should be reduced.

E. Kaizen costing also has been criticized for placing enormous pressure on employees to reduce every possible cost. To address the problem, some Japanese automobile companies use a grace, or cost sustainment, period in manufacturing just before a new model is introduced. This allows employees the chance to learn about any new procedures before the company imposes Kaizen targets on them.

Learning Objective 4: Understand the importance and process of controlling the costs of nonconformance of products to established quality standards.

V. Cost of Nonconformance (Quality)

A. The **cost of nonconformance** (CONC) is a measure of the cost to an organization of poor quality in its products, processes, and services.

B. Quality is determined by two major factors:

1. Satisfying customer expectations regarding the attributes and performance of a product, such as its functionality and features.

2. Ensuring that the technical aspects of the product's design and performance conform to standards from the manufacturer's perspective.

C. The ISO 9000 Standards, developed in Europe in 1987, provide globally-recognized quality standards for products and services. Exhibit 13-8 provides details on the ISO guidelines, consisting of five standards.

D. The Japanese equivalent of the ISO Guidelines is Japanese Industrial Standard Z8101-1981. The standard specifies that effective quality control results from the cooperation of everyone in the organization, and all functional areas of an organization must adhere to the standard.

E. In the United States, the American Quality Control Society has developed its own standards, Q90-Q94. Exhibit 13-9 discusses these in more detail.

F. Cost of Quality Categories

1. **Prevention costs** are incurred to ensure that companies produce products according to quality standards. Examples include quality engineering, training employees in methods to maintain quality, and statistical process control.

2. **Appraisal costs** typically are those related to inspecting products to make sure that they meet both internal and external customer requirements. Examples include inspection of incoming materials, process control monitoring, and product quality audits.

3. **Internal failure costs** occur when the manufacturing process produces a defective component or product and detects the failure internally. Examples include the cost of downtime in production as a result of discovering defectives, and scrap and rework costs.

4. **External failure costs** are those incurred if a customer discovers a defective product or component once it has left the factory. Examples include warranty costs, service calls, product liability recalls, and product liability lawsuits.

Exhibit 13-10 provides more examples of quality-related costs.

Exhibit 13-11 illustrates a Quality Cost Report. Note that the four cost categories are listed together with their annual cost and the percentage of sales that each cost represents. Exhibit 13-12 shows the cost of quality categories comparatively with the actual and desired trends.

Learning Objective 5: Understand a model for benchmarking the best practices of other organizations.

VI. Benchmarking

A. Benchmarking typically consists of five stages. These stages are listed below and shown in Exhibit 13-13, which also lists factors to consider at each stage.

1. Internal study and preliminary competitive analyses

2. Develop long-term commitment to the benchmarking project and coalesce the benchmarking team

3. Identify benchmarking partners

4. Information gathering- and sharing-methods

5. Take action to meet or exceed the benchmark

Exhibit 13-13 provides many specific examples of factors that can be benchmarked in each of the five stages above.

Learning Objective 6: Show how to apply the benchmarking model to learning about advances in management accounting methods.

B. Benchmarking and Management Accounting Methods

1. Exhibit 13-14 illustrates how the following management accounting methods can be benchmarked with those of other organizations:

    a. Total life cycle costing.

    b. Target costing.

    c. Kaizen costing.

    d. Quality costing.

2. For each of the above methods, the organizational structure and culture play a key role.

Exhibit 13-14 lists important factors to benchmark for each of the management accounting methods above, providing a review of some central features of each method.

PRACTICE TEST QUESTIONS AND PROBLEMS

True/False

____ 1. The greatest opportunity to influence product costs and product design occurs in the manufacturing cycle.

____ 2. The post-sale service and disposal cycle overlaps with the manufacturing cycle.

____ 3. Total life cycle costing of a product includes costs incurred before, during, and after the manufacturing cycle.

____ 4. Manufacturing organizations should focus their attention primarily on manufacturing costs, because manufacturing costs invariably constitute the largest percentage of total costs.

____ 5. Benchmarking (or performance) gaps are determined only for quantitative measures related to manufacturing processes.

____ 6. Kaizen costing and target costing both have a mission of cost reduction.

____ 7. Kaizen costing is virtually identical to standard costing.

____ 8. Industry leaders do not need to benchmark.

____ 9. Quality cost reports generally list the four cost categories, together with their annual cost and the percentage of sales that each cost represents.

____ 10. An organization developing benchmarking as it adopts a total life cycle costing approach should expect that a short-term commitment to benchmarking will be adequate.

Multiple-Choice

1. Which of the following is NOT part of the RD&E cycle?

   (a) Kaizen costing
   (b) Value engineering
   (c) Target costing
   (d) Market research

2. Traditional cost reduction involves all of the following, EXCEPT

   (a) market research into customer requirements.
   (b) estimation of product cost.
   (c) obtaining prices from suppliers.
   (d) value engineering.

3. Which of the following is NOT one of the four cost of quality categories?

   (a) Appraisal costs
   (b) Internal failure costs
   (c) Prevention costs
   (d) Benchmarking costs

4. The cost of which of the following is an example of an appraisal cost in the cost of quality framework?

   (a) Maintenance of test equipment
   (b) Statistical process control
   (c) Supplier certification
   (d) Product liability recalls

5. Which of the following is NOT true about benchmarking?

   (a) It requires that organizational members understand their current operations and approaches to conducting business.
   (b) It looks externally to practices of other organizations for guidance on improving.
   (c) It is often highly cost-effective.
   (d) Only manufacturing processes can be benchmarked.

6. Which of the following is NOT an example of cooperative benchmarking?

   (a) Relying on aggregate or average data from industry trade associations.
   (b) Purchasing information from a database operator who collects and edits the information prior to revealing it to users; the identity of the source of the data often is not revealed.
   (c) Hiring an outside consultant to act as a liaison among firms engaged in benchmarking.
   (d) Benchmarking by meeting with others to discuss methods.

7. Which of the following is NOT a concern about target costing?

   (a) It can lead to conflicts among organization members.
   (b) Employees experience a great amount of pressure to meet goals, leading to burnout.
   (c) The marketing researchers in the organization will be unhappy because they have no role in the target costing process.
   (d) Time to market may be slowed because of repeated cycles of attempts reduce costs.

8. Which of the following is NOT true about a standard costing system?

   (a) It is based on a cost control concept.
   (b) It assumes stability in the current manufacturing process.
   (c) The goal is to meet cost performance standards.
   (d) It assumes production workers have the best knowledge to reduce costs.

9. Which of the following is NOT true about quality standards?

   (a) The Japanese use Industrial Standard Z8101-1981.
   (b) The American Quality Control Society has developed quality standards known as the Q Series of Quality Standards.
   (c) The ISO, headquartered in Europe, developed the ISO 9000 series of standards.
   (d) Only European countries can be certified under the ISO 9000 guidelines.

10. Which of the following would NOT be a result of the value engineering process?

    (a) A change in the product design
    (b) Replacement of some materials used in production
    (c) Redesign of manufacturing processes
    (d) Setting of a preliminary target cost for the product

Completion

1. ____________ ____________ ____________ ____________ provides information for managers to understand and manage costs through a product's design, development, manufacturing, marketing, distribution, maintenance, service, and disposal stages.

2. During the RD&E stage of the total life cycle of a product that requires discrete manufacturing processes and reasonably short product life cycles, __________ ____________ is used as a method of cost planning that focuses on reducing costs.

3. The ________ ____ __________________ is a measure of the cost to an organization of poor quality in its products, processes, and services.

4. In the _______-_______ method of pricing, an expected or desired profit margin is added to the expected product cost to arrive at the selling price.

5. The ________ _______________ process examines each component of a product to determine whether it is possible to reduce costs while maintaining functionality and performance.

6. _______________ means making improvements to a process through small, incremental amounts.

7. The four-category quality cost framework results from experience that shows it is much less expensive to ______________ defects than to _____________ and _______________ them after they have occurred.

8. In Kaizen costing, the _________ ________________ _______, which is the ratio of the target reduction amount divided by the cost base, is applied to all variable costs.

9. The three broad classes of information on which firms benchmark are ________________ benchmarking, ____________________ benchmarking, and ________________ benchmarking.

10. Benchmarking management accounting methods is becoming more widespread as organizations increasingly view the methods as a source of ______________ ________________.

Problems

1. Traditional cost-plus pricing has been labeled "cost up/price up," and target costing has been labeled "price down/cost down." Explain why these labels might be appropriate.

2. The data below have been gathered on annual quality costs at KWT Company for 1996:

Inspection of Incoming Materials	$ 800,000
Maintenance of Test Equipment	400,000
Net Cost of Scrap	200,000
Process Control Monitoring	1,000,000
Product Liability Recalls	500,000
Product Quality Audits	450,000
Quality Engineering	300,000
Rework Costs	600,000
Statistical Process Control	150,000
Supplier Certification	10,000
Warranty Claims	400,000

Total sales for 1996 were $25,000,000.

REQUIRED:

Prepare a cost of quality report using the data above. What recommendations do you have for KWT Company?

SOLUTIONS TO PRACTICE TEST QUESTIONS AND PROBLEMS

True/False

1. False. Product costs and product design are primarily set in the RD&E cycle.

2. True. The post-sale service and disposal cycle begins once the first unit of product is in the hands of a customer.

3. True. Total life cycle costing of a product includes costs incurred before, during, and after the manufacturing cycle.

4. False. Focusing only on manufacturing costs could cause organizations to ignore a significant proportion of RD&E or service and disposal costs.

5. False. Benchmarking gap analysis can include more qualitative measures and measures not directly associated with manufacturing processes.

6. True. Kaizen costing and target costing both have a mission of cost reduction. Kaizen costing occurs during the manufacturing stage, and target costing occurs during the RD&E stage.

7. False. Kaizen costing and standard costing are quite distinct (see Exhibit 13-7).

8. False. Industry leaders may benchmark because of their commitment to continuous improvement or in order to remain competitive. Moreover, industry leaders with respect to product lines can also benchmark processes not directly related to the product lines.

9. True. Quality cost reports generally list the absolute costs and the relative costs (as a percentage of sales). Separating the costs into the four categories allows management to see how the quality costs or costs of poor quality are distributed.

10. False. Adopting a total life cycle costing approach involves significant organizational change that can take several years. Consequently, the commitment to benchmarking should be long-term.

Multiple-Choice

1. a. Kaizen costing focuses on the manufacturing cycle.

2. d. Value engineering is associated with target costing.

3. d. The fourth category of costs is external failure costs.

4. a. The cost of maintenance of test equipment is an appraisal cost; costs of statistical process control and supplier certification are prevention costs; costs of product liability recalls are external failure costs.

5. d. Nonmanufacturing processes can be benchmarked. For example, management accounting methods can be benchmarked.

6. a. Relying on aggregate or average data from industry trade associations is an example of unilateral benchmarking.

7. c. Market research is a vital component of the target costing process.

8. d. In traditional standard costing, it is assumed that managers and engineers have the best knowledge to reduce costs. The assumption that production workers have the best knowledge to reduce costs is characteristic of Kaizen costing.

9. d. The ISO 9000 guidelines are international standards.

10. d. A preliminary target cost is set *before* the value engineering process begins.

Completion

1. Total life cycle costing
2. target costing
3. cost of nonconformance
4. cost plus
5. value engineering
6. Kaizen
7. prevent, detect, repair
8. target reduction rate
9. product, functional (or process), strategic
10. competitive advantage

Problems

1. In traditional cost-plus pricing, estimated product costs plus an expected or desired profit margin yields the projected price. Therefore, if product cost is high, the projected selling price will also be high. That is, as "costs go up, prices go up."

   In target costing, a target selling price is determined, based on perceptions of the value of the product to the customer, and on market conditions. The target profit margin is then subtracted from the target selling price to arrive at a target cost. Therefore, if perceptions are that prices must be relatively low, the product cost must also be relatively low in order to achieve the desired profit margin. That is, as "prices go down, costs must go down."

2.

	Annual Cost	Cost/ Sales
Prevention Costs:		
Quality Engineering	$ 300,000	0.0120
Statistical Process Control	150,000	0.0060
Supplier Certification	10,000	0.0004
	$ 460,000	0.0184
Appraisal Costs:		
Inspection of Incoming Materials	$ 800,000	0.0320
Maintenance of Test Equipment	400,000	0.0160
Product Quality Audits	450,000	0.0180
Process Control Monitoring	1,000,000	0.0400
	$2,650,000	0.1060
Internal Failure Costs:		
Rework Costs	$ 600,000	0.0240
Net Cost of Scrap	200,000	0.0080
	$ 800,000	0.0320
External Failure Costs:		
Warranty Claims	$ 400,000	0.0160
Product Liability Recalls	500,000	0.0200
	$ 900,000	0.0360

Although KWT Company has a relatively low proportion of prevention, internal failure, and external failure costs, it has high proportion of appraisal costs. KWT should consider shifting some of the emphasis away from appraisal, to prevention. For example, inspection of incoming materials could be greatly reduced by a more aggressive program of supplier certification.

Notes and Questions

Chapter 14

Compensation Issues

CENTRAL FOCUS AND LEARNING OBJECTIVES

After reading this chapter, you will be able to

1. understand the role of motivation in organizations.
2. discuss the significant elements of two influential theories of motivation.
3. understand how organizations tie individual objectives to organizational objectives.
4. explain several approaches to rewarding performance and the nature of intrinsic and extrinsic rewards.
5. identify what makes effective reward systems.
6. explain the broad types of monetary rewards that organizations use.

REVIEW OF KEY TERMS AND CONCEPTS

Learning Objective 1: Understand the role of motivation in organizations.

Learning Objective 2: Discuss the significant elements of two influential theories of motivation.

I. The Role of Compensation in Organizational Control

Recall that *control* refers to the tools and methods an organization uses to keep it on track toward achieving its objectives. An important element of control is motivating employees to pursue the organization's interests. Compensation is a highly visible and extremely important factor affecting motivation. This chapter discusses a number of central issues relating to compensation, beginning with two well-known theories of individual motivation.

A. **Two-factor theory,** developed by Herzberg, argues that there are two groups of factors, with different roles, that motivate individual behavior.

1. **Hygiene factors** are those necessary to provide an appropriate environment for motivation, rather than motivation itself. Base pay serves as a hygiene factor.

2. **Satisfier factors** provide motivation when the environment for motivation has been properly prepared. Any discretionary part of pay that the employee perceives as recognition of performance serves as a satisfier factor.

B. Vroom's Expectancy Theory

Expectancy theory argues that motivation is a product of expectancy, instrumentality, and valence.

1. **Expectancy** is the relationship that a person perceives between effort and skill, and whether these will achieve the targeted performance.

2. **Instrumentality** is the relationship between measured performance and the outcomes provided to individuals.

3. A **valence** is the value that a person assigns to the outcomes provided by the organization as a result of formal performance measurement.

C. A **motivation system** is a performance measurement and reward system that provides employee benefits or recognition based on measured performance.

Exhibits 14-1 and 14-2 illustrate Herzberg's and Vroom's theories. What are the key differences?

Exhibit 14-3 summarizes the perspective that the major role of the motivation system is to tie the individual's objectives to those of the organization.

Learning Objective 3: Understand how organizations tie individual objectives to organizational objectives.

Learning Objective 4: Explain several approaches to rewarding performance and the nature of intrinsic and extrinsic rewards.

II. Factors Affecting Individual Motivation

Organizations use two broad categories of rewards to motivate people:

A. **Intrinsic rewards** are those relating to the nature of the organization and the design of the job, that people experience without the intervention of anyone else. These rewards come from inside the individual and include satisfaction and feelings of accomplishment.

B. **Extrinsic rewards** are those based on assessed performance. These include trips, financial rewards, and employee awards.

C. There is much debate about what types and mix of rewards (intrinsic versus extrinsic rewards) should be used. On the one hand, some argue that not enough emphasis is placed on developing an environment from which intrinsic rewards for individuals can be derived. On the other hand, some claim that extrinsic rewards are the most motivating types of rewards and that people respond best to money and external recognition that is based on their performance. Each organization must decide on the type of work environment it would like to develop and the mix of both types of rewards.

III. Rewards Based on Performance

Incentive compensation, or pay-for-performance, is a system that provides rewards for performance to motivate achieving, or exceeding, measured performance targets.

A. Rewards can be based on *absolute performance,* as in piece-rate incentive schemes for the number of good products produced.

B. Rewards also can be based on performance relative to a plan or to a comparable group. For example, a *relative performance* plan might pay a bonus to the top insurance salesperson each month.

Learning Objective 5: Identify what makes effective reward systems.

IV. Effective Performance Measurement and Reward Systems

A. If the organization has decided to reward performance, six broad characteristics should be considered to ensure that the performance measurement system will be effective.

1. Individuals must understand their jobs and the reward system, and know how to improve their performance. Further, the issue of controllability is important.

2. A careful choice must be made about whether the performance measurement system measures the employee's inputs, outputs, or a mix of the two.

3. The performance measurement system should reflect the organization's critical success factors, and measure performance across a set of balanced and comprehensive measures, as proposed in the balanced scorecard.

4. The reward system must set clear standards for performance.

5. The measurement system must measure the objects of measurement systematically and accurately.

6. Where appropriate, incentives should consider rewarding groups, rather than individuals.

Were all of the above conditions present in the last job (full-time or part-time) that you had?

B. Conditions Favoring Incentive Compensation

Incentive compensation seems to work best in decentralized systems where employees are empowered and can use their skill and authority to react to situations and make decisions.

C. Incentive Compensation and Employee Responsibility

An employee's compensation should reflect the nature of his or her responsibilities. For instance, those who work in daily operations should have rewards that are tied to short-term measures, such as customer service; those who work on intermediate-term projects should be rewarded based on meeting budgets. Finally, those who work on long-term projects should be rewarded on measures such as long-term growth or process improvements.

D. Rewarding Outcomes

Employees provide two types of inputs to an organization. These are time and skill. Incentive system designers usually look to the outputs of employees as measures of how employees use their inputs on the job. As employees bring more skill and experience to a job, they are rewarded with some form of knowledge-based pay. Thus, employees are encouraged to keep upgrading their skills.

E. Managing Incentive Compensation Plans

There is controversy over the management of compensation plans, especially at the senior executive level. The criticism is that senior executives have been overpaid for mediocre performance. This perceived unfairness has tended to discourage lower-level employees' beliefs that incentive compensation systems are equitable.

Learning Objective 6: Explain the broad types of monetary rewards that organizations use.

V. Types of Incentive Compensation Plans

Compensation plans can be grouped into two broad classes. The first relies on internal measures (usually provided by the management accounting system), and the second relies on the organization's share price in the stock market.

A. A **cash bonus** (also called a lump-sum reward or merit pay), is a cash award based on some measured performance. Cash bonuses can be based on individual or group performance. The bonus can be fixed in amount and triggered when performance exceeds a target, or can be proportional to the level of performance.

B. **Profit sharing** is a cash bonus system where the total amount available for distribution as cash bonuses is a function of the organization's, or an organization unit's, reported profit. Thus, profit-sharing is a group incentive plan.

C. **Gain sharing** is another group incentive system where the total amount available for distribution as cash bonuses is a function of performance relative to some target (usually the difference between the actual and the target level of labor cost).

The three most widely used gain sharing programs are:

1. Improshare (Improved Productivity Sharing).

   The bonus pool is determined by calculating the difference between the target level of labor cost, given the level of production, and the actual labor cost.

2. Scanlon Plan

   First a base ratio is calculated using past data.

   $$\text{Base ratio} = \frac{\text{Payroll costs}}{\text{Value of goods or services produced}}$$

   In any period in which the ratio of payroll costs are less than the base ratio, the labor savings are added to the bonus pool.

3. Rucker Plan

   The Rucker plan also works on a ratio based on past data.

   $$\text{Rucker standard} = \frac{\text{Payroll costs}}{\text{Production value}}$$

   where production value = (net sales - inventory change - materials and supplies used).

   Similar to the Scanlon plan, when actual labor costs are less than the Rucker standard, its employees receive a bonus.

D. A **stock option** is a right to purchase a stated number of the organization's shares at a stipulated price (the option price).

   The general idea behind stock options is to motivate employees to act in the long-run interests of the organization by taking actions and making decisions that will increase the organization's market value.

E. Other Incentive Plans

The two plans below reward employees for information developed and communicated to organization planners.

1. The Soviet incentive plan was designed and used in the former Soviet Union to coordinate the activities of production units (called enterprises). The plan focused on extracting reliable production estimates from experts.

2. The Groves mechanism uses a mix of organization and segment rewards to provide an incentive for an expert to provide unbiased information.

PRACTICE TEST QUESTIONS AND PROBLEMS

True/False

____ 1. Herzberg's Two-Factor Theory incorporates the concept of instrumentality.

____ 2. A valence is a value assigned by the individual to the outcomes.

____ 3. Receiving a plaque for one's performance is an extrinsic reward.

____ 4. An example of a reward based on absolute performance is paying a salesperson a bonus for exceeding the average performance of the sales group.

____ 5. Incentive compensation systems work best in organizations in which employees have the skill and authority to make decisions.

____ 6. The rewards of employees who manage daily operations should be tied to short-term performance measures.

____ 7. Most experts believe that organizations using incentive compensation should restrict the participation in the plans to only senior executives.

____ 8. Studies have shown that monetary compensation is the only factor that affects employees' motivation.

____ 9. A cash bonus is also called merit pay.

____ 10. A stock option is the right to purchase a unit of the organization's stock at a specified price, called the option price.

Multiple Choice

1. In Herzberg's Two-Factor Theory of motivation, base pay is

   (a) an expectancy.
   (b) a hygiene factor.
   (c) a satisfier factor.
   (d) a valence.

2. In Vroom's Expectancy Theory, motivation is

   (a) (Expectancy × Instrumentality) + Valence.
   (b) Expectancy + (Instrumentality × Valence).
   (c) Expectancy + Instrumentality + Valence.
   (d) Expectancy × Instrumentality × Valence.

3. Which of the following is NOT an intrinsic reward?

   (a) Job satisfaction
   (b) Opportunity for personal development
   (c) Being named employee of the month
   (d) Pride of accomplishment

4. Which of the following is NOT needed in the effective design of a performance measurement and reward system?

   (a) Always design the reward system based on the performance of the individual.
   (b) Make sure all employees know their jobs.
   (c) Make sure employees understand the relationship between performance improvements and their effects on rewards.
   (d) Design the system to monitor and reward the organization's critical success factors.

5. Employees bring two major types of inputs to an organization that forms the basis of their compensation. These are:

   (a) effort, attitude.
   (b) time, personality.
   (c) effort, personality.
   (d) time, skill.

6. Which of the following is NOT a reason that designing compensations contracts is difficult?

   (a) Outcomes often reflect the joint effect of a decision and environmental uncertainty.
   (b) Outcomes are often the result of the activities of many people.
   (c) There is considerable disagreement among experts about the precise effect of compensation on motivation.
   (d) A compensation contract for an individual can be based only on outcomes that the individual controls.

7. Which of the following is NOT true about incentive plans designed to motivate employees to develop and communicate accurate information to organization planners?

   (a) The Soviet incentive system was designed to obtain accurate forecasts to support central planning.
   (b) Incentive schemes that reward information provision are rarely found in practice.
   (c) The Groves mechanism uses a mix of organization and segment rewards to provide an incentive for an expert to provide unbiased information.
   (d) The Soviet incentive system provides an incentive to provide an honest estimate and to work as hard as possible to achieve the target production level.

8. In the Scanlon plan, the base ratio is

   (a) Payroll costs/Value of production or service.
   (b) Payroll costs/inventory turnover.
   (c) Net cash inflow/Value of production or service.
   (d) Net cash inflow/Net sales.

9. Under the Scanlon plan, Ideal Company's base ratio is 0.25. If payroll costs are $5,000,000 and the value of production is $18,000,000, how much money is added to the bonus pool?

   (a) $ 500,000.
   (b) $3,250,000.
   (c) $ 0.
   (d) $4,500,000.

10. Stock options are usually available for

(a) all employees of a firm.
(b) middle managers and higher level executives.
(c) operations manager and higher level managers.
(d) senior executives.

Completion

1. _____________ factors relate to the job context and define the environment of the individual's work.

2. ______________ factors relate to the job content and define how the person feels about his or her job.

3. Victor Vroom developed a model of motivation that he called _________________ ________________.

4. _________________ rewards relate to the nature of the organization and the design of the job that people experience, and they come from inside the individual.

5. Incentive compensation systems, or ________-________-________________ systems, are reward systems that provide monetary rewards based on measured results.

6. In Vroom's theory, ______________________ is the relationship between the individual's measured performance and the outcomes provided by the organization, such as pay for performance.

7. ____________ ______________ is a group incentive system for distributing cash bonuses, where the total amount available for distribution as cash bonuses is based on reported profit.

8. ____________________ is a group incentive system for distributing cash bonuses, where the total amount available is a function of performance relative to some target.

9. Improshare stands for _________________ __________________ ________________.

10. The Rucker standard is the ratio of ______________ __________ to _________________ ___________.

Problems

1. You are charged with designing an incentive compensation scheme for a major airline. Fill in the following table listing the most appropriate incentive and the kind(s) of behavior that should be rewarded.

Type of Employee	Type of Incentive	Behavior to Reward
Senior Executive		
Pilot		
Flight Attendant		
Complaint Office Manager		
Maintenance Worker		

2. Contrast and compare the differences in cash bonuses, profit-sharing schemes, gain sharing systems, and stock options.

SOLUTIONS TO PRACTICE TEST QUESTIONS AND PROBLEMS

True/False

1. False. Victor Vroom's expectancy theory incorporates the concept of instrumentality.

2. True. A valence is a value assigned by the individual to the outcomes.

3. True. A plaque is an example of an extrinsic reward.

4. False. Paying a salesperson a bonus for exceeding the average performance of the sales group is an example of a reward based on *relative performance*.

5. True. Incentive compensation systems do work best in organizations in which employees have the skill and authority to make decisions.

6. True. For managing daily activities, using short-term rewards is the most appropriate thing to do.

7. False. Many experts agree that all employees should participate in one plan or another within the same organization.

8. False. Nonmonetary factors, such as the organization's general management style, and various forms of special recognition, also motivate people.

9. True. Another name for a cash bonus is merit pay.

10. True. A stock option is the right to purchase a unit of the organization's stock at a specified price, called the option price.

Multiple-Choice

1. b. In Herzberg's theory, base pay is a hygiene factor.

2. d. In Vroom's theory,
   Motivation = Expectancy × Instrumentality × Valence.

3. c. Being named employee of the month is an extrinsic reward.

4. a. Reward systems should be based on the performance of individuals or groups, depending on the situation.

5. d. The two major *inputs* on which employees' compensation is based are time and skill. Of course, compensation can be based on other measures, such as individual or group *outputs.*

6. d. Compensation can also be based on inputs, group measures, or relative performance.

7. b. Incentive schemes that reward information provision are rarely found in practice. However, as organizations increasingly attempt to motivate the development of expert knowledge for the benefit of the organization, such incentive schemes may become more common.

8. a. In the Scanlon plan, the base ratio is: Payroll costs/Value of production or service.

9. c. Under the Scanlon plan, money is added to the bonus pool only if the ratio of labor costs to production value is less than the base ratio. In this case, the ratio in the current period is $5,000,000/$18,000,000 or 0.28 which is higher than the base ratio of 0.25. Thus, no money is added to the bonus pool for the Ideal Company.

   Equivalently, as demonstrated in the textbook, one can compute the potential amount to be added to the bonus pool as: (value of production this period × base ratio) - actual payroll costs = ($18,000,000 × 0.25) - $5,000,000 = $4,500,000 = $5,000,000 < 0. Therefore, no money will be added to the bonus pool.

10. d. Stock options are usually available for senior executives only.

Completion

1. Hygiene
2. Satisfier
3. Expectancy Theory

4. Intrinsic

5. pay for performance

6. instrumentality

7. Profit sharing

8. Gainsharing

9. Improved Productivity Sharing

10. payroll costs, production value

Problems

1. There are many ways to design an incentive scheme. The table below illustrates some options. Bonuses listed in the table are based on how well each employee does on the behaviors that should be rewarded in the third column.

Type of Employee	Type of Incentive	Behavior to Reward
Senior Executive	Stock options; bonus	Leadership ability
Pilot	Market wage plus bonus	On-time arrival and safe flights
Flight Attendant	Market wage plus bonus	Customer satisfaction
Complaint Office Manager	Market wage plus bonus	Customer satisfaction
Maintenance Worker	Market wage plus bonus	Number of error-free flights

2. Cash bonuses are payments of cash based on performance related to a standard or target. Commonly, when a target is met, the bonus is awarded. Cash bonuses are one-time awards that are not part of an employee's base pay. Profit sharing is a cash bonus that reflects the performance of a unit within an organization or the performance of the entire organization. Thus, profit sharing is focused on a group's short-term performance on a specific indicator. Gainsharing is a system that awards cash bonuses based on a group or team achieving beyond a set standard or target. The target is usually based on a base-period performance indicator. Examples of gainsharing include Improshare, Scanlon plans, and Rucker plans. Finally, stock options are usually used to motivate and focus senior executives in organizations. Stock options are intended to motivate senior executives to consider the long-term performance of their organization. The theory goes that as the value of the organization increases, so will the market price of the stock. In turn, the market price of the stock will exceed the option price of the stock.

Notes and Questions

Chapter 15

Management Accounting and Control System Design: Behavioral Factors and Change Management

CENTRAL FOCUS AND LEARNING OBJECTIVES

After reading this chapter, you will be able to

1. discuss managerial approaches to motivation and, in particular, the human resources model.
2. identify the characteristics of a well-designed management accounting and control system (MACS) and the links among the concepts of motivation, ethics, control, and performance.
3. evaluate the behavioral consequences of a poorly designed MACS.
4. understand the behavioral implications of implementing a new MACS or changing a current MACS.

REVIEW OF KEY TERMS AND CONCEPTS

I. Goals of a Management Accounting and Control System (MACS)

A. **Planning** for the future.

B. **Monitoring** events in the external environment.

C. **Measuring** and **recording** the results of activities occurring inside the organization.

D. **Motivating** individuals and groups who are affected by and who affect the MACS.

E. **Evaluating the performance** of individuals and groups in the organization.

Because people are involved with each of these goals, there is a strong connection between management accounting methods and systems and the study of human behavior. A MACS design must consider how humans affect and are affected by management accounting information.

Learning Objective 1: Discuss managerial approaches to motivation and, in particular, the human resources model.

II. Managerial Approaches to Motivation

In contrast to the psychological models of individual motivation discussed in Chapter 14, there are three major managerial approaches to motivation.

A. **Scientific management:** a school of motivation in which people were viewed as finding work objectionable, motivated only by money, and having little knowledge to contribute to the organization.

B. **Human relations movement:** a model of human motivation that considers employees' many needs and aspirations at work, and motivation by things other than money.

C. **The human resources model:** an approach to human motivation that emphasizes that individuals do not find work objectionable, that they have knowledge to contribute, and that they are highly creative and responsible. With this model, managers often focus on three aspects of employee motivation.

1. Direction: where an employee focuses attention at work.

2. Intensity: the level of effort expended.

3. Persistence: the duration of time spent on the task or job.

When employees have aligned their individual goals with those of the organization, **goal congruence** is said to occur.

How do the three managerial approaches to motivation differ? This chapter uses the human resources model as the basis for understanding the design of a MACS.

Learning Objective 2: Identify the characteristics of a well-designed management accounting and control system (MACS) and the links among the concepts of motivation, ethics, control, and performance.

III. Five Key Characteristics of a MACS

A. The **multiple perspectives approach** provides for a consistent, organization-wide management accounting system that also allows for local input and tailoring, and fosters continuous improvement.

B. A system that reinforces the **ethical responsibilities** of all firm employees. Most organizations attempt to avoid ethical dilemmas by developing a code of ethics.

1. The **hierarchy of ethical principles** listed below captures a broad array of ethical considerations.

a. Legal rules.

b. Societal norms.

c. Professional codes (CPAs, and CMAs, for example).

d. Organizational or group norms.

e. Personal norms.

2. Dealing with Ethical Conflicts

Different kinds of conflicts can arise for employees in an organization. These include:

a. conflicts between individual and organizational values.

b. conflicts between the organization's stated and practiced values. Alternative four in the textbook, *delay taking action and work with respected leaders in the organization to change the discrepancy* is one that is often recommended.

3. Elements of an Effective Ethical Control System

a. A **statement** of the organization's values and code of ethics that is stated in practical terms, and that uses examples.

b. A clear statement of the employee's **ethical responsibilities** for every job description.

c. Adequate **training** to help employees identify ethical dilemmas in practice and learn how to deal with those dilemmas.

d. Evidence that senior management expects organization members to **adhere** to its code of ethics.

e. Evidence that employees can make ethical decisions, or report violations of the organization's stated ethics **without fear of reprisals** from superiors, subordinates, or peers in the organization.

f. Providing for an ongoing **internal audit** of the efficacy of the organization's ethical control system.

Review the steps in the Decision Model for Resolving Ethical Issues in Table 15.1. Can you think of a situation to which you can apply the steps?

C. The development and use of both **quantitative and qualitative measures** in a timely fashion for control, motivation, and performance evaluation.

   1. **Quantitative financial measures** include cost, profit, and net income.

   2. **Quantitative nonfinancial measures** include yield, cycle time, schedule adherence, and defectives.

   3. **Qualitative measures** include image and reputation.

D. The **participation and empowerment of employees** in system design and improvements, and continuous education of employees in understanding how the system functions and how the information can be interpreted meaningfully.

   1. **Employee empowerment** means providing employees the ability to affect their work environment through more discretion and autonomy.

   2. **Participation** in decision-making refers to a decision-making process in which all parties jointly decide on a plan of action.

E. Development of mechanisms such as **reward systems** tied to performance, to promote motivation and goal congruence between the organization and employees, thereby reducing dysfunctional behavior.

Before going on, be sure that you understand the five key characteristics of a MACS.

Learning Objective 3: Evaluate the behavioral consequences of a poorly designed MACS.

IV. Behavioral Consequences of Poorly Designed Systems

A MACS will be said to be **poorly designed** if it lacks at least one of the five key MACS characteristics. A poorly designed MACS can lead to reduced motivation and increased nongoal-congruent behavior. (Recall that goal congruence is the alignment of an individual's and the organization's goals.) Three types of **nongoal-congruent behavior** are listed below.

A. **Smoothing** occurs when an employee alters the preplanned flow of information without altering actual behavior.

B. **Gaming** occurs when an employee alters his or her planned actions as a result of a particular kind of performance indicator. Building **budget slack** (see Chapter 9), or requesting excess resources above what are needed to accomplish the goals set forth in the budget, is an example of gaming.

C. **Data falsification** is the act of knowingly falsifying information.

Describe the differences among the three methods of nongoal-congruent behavior.

Learning Objective 4: Understand the behavioral implications of implementing a new MACS or changing a current MACS.

V. Behavioral Considerations when Implementing a New MACS

A. There are two different phases of implementation:

1. Phase 1 involves designing and building the new MACS.

2. Phase 2 involves using the MACS.

B. Considerations in Phase 1 Implementation

1. Before changes to the MACS are made, organizations often use **cooperative benchmarking** to compare and borrow information from other organizations on best practices in designing a MACS.

2. **Senior management support** may be the most critical variable in implementation success

3. A **change champion** is an individual who takes the initiative and risk to develop a new management accounting system. The champion also coordinates a **multifunctional team** to help provide information and support.

C. Considerations in Phase 2 Implementation

1. The **change process** consists of the procedures and actions by which change is implemented.

2. Knowledge of **organizational culture** is a key element in changing systems. Organizational culture can be defined as the mindset of organizational participants, including goals, values, and attitudes. There are many types of cultures, including:

   a. **strong functional cultures** with well-defined goals and values, and a great deal of employee involvement and goal congruence.

   b. **strong dysfunctional cultures** that are usually characterized by top-down control, little employee involvement, and very little goal congruence. However, performance may be high if employees work hard out of fear.

   c. **ill-defined cultures** in which employees do not have a strong sense of corporate mission. Goal congruence is usually low.

3. **Knowledge of current manufacturing and service practices and control methods** is another key element in changing systems. Organizations that have tried to implement JIT systems have often not taken into account

the difference between primary and secondary control systems, and as a result have met with resistance

a. **Primary control** is a method of control in which employees further their own ends by trying to influence their environment.

b. **Secondary control** is a method of control in which employees adapt themselves to their environment, rather than trying to change the environment.

4. **Resistance to change,** often a major stumbling block, can arise when an employee refuses to accept the changes brought about in an organization. Some of these reasons are:

   a. People often exhibit a defense response when they are set in their ways or worried about change.

   b. Change can be costly in terms of lost compensation for some employees and the amount of lost time during the change.

   c. Change can shift the power base in the organization.

   d. **Resistance to ABC/ABM**, in particular, may occur because:

      i. change to ABC may affect a unit's assessed profitability.

      ii. activity analysis can reveal how employees are really spending their time.

      iii. some employees associate ABC/ABM with cost cutting and they are afraid that they will lose their jobs.

   e. The scope of change is initially too large.

5. **Commitment** is the implicit pledging of organizational participants to a course of action. **Continuous education** is a commitment on the part of the organization to provide educational programs for employees on an on-going basis.

6. **Compensation** consists of financial incentives to promote desired behavior (see Chapter 14).

Can you describe the key factors the decision-maker should be concerned with before changing to a new MACS?

PRACTICE TEST QUESTIONS AND PROBLEMS

True/False

____ 1. The scientific management school of motivation assumes that individuals have a great deal of knowledge and information to contribute to the organization, and that they are highly creative and responsible.

____ 2. Three key aspects of motivation are direction, intensity, and pertinence.

____ 3. The multiple perspectives approach to MACS design requires only a consistent, global, technical structure.

____ 4. One element of an ethical control system is a clear statement of the employees' ethical responsibilities for every job description.

____ 5. Ethical dilemmas at work can be resolved only in a court of law.

____ 6. Developing and using both quantitative and qualitative information is a key characteristic of a well-designed MACS.

____ 7. Gaming is an example of goal-congruent behavior.

____ 8. In implementing a new MACS, Phase 1 involves designing and building the new MACS, and Phase 2 involves using the new MACS.

____ 9. Three general types of organizational cultures are strong functional, strong dysfunctional, and well-defined.

____ 10. If an employee observes management engaged in unethical behavior, the best course of action for the employee is to resign and make the issue public.

Multiple-Choice

1. The three management approaches to motivation are

   (a) Vroom's expectancy theory, Herzberg's two-factor theory, and the human relations movement.
   (b) Herzberg's two-factor theory, scientific management, and human resources model.
   (c) scientific management, human resources model, and Vroom's expectancy theory.
   (d) scientific management, human relations movement, and human resources model.

2. Which of the following is NOT a characteristic of a well-designed MACS?

   (a) The system is designed from the point of view of top management.
   (b) Employees can participate and are empowered.
   (c) An ethical code of conduct is incorporated.
   (d) Reward systems are tied to performance.

3. The following are all characteristics of the human resources view of human motivation, EXCEPT

   (a) people do not find work objectionable.
   (b) people want to participate in developing objectives.
   (c) people's primary motivation at work is to make as much money as possible.
   (d) people have a great deal of knowledge to contribute to the organization.

4. The elements of an effective ethical control system include all of the following, EXCEPT

   (a) a statement of the organization's values and code of ethics.
   (b) a sworn affidavit by each employee that he or she will not violate the code.
   (c) a clear statement of the employee's ethical responsibilities.
   (d) a statement by management that outlines the consequences for violating the code.

5. An example of a qualitative performance measure is

(a) on-time delivery.
(b) speed to market.
(c) output per hour.
(d) warmth of the hospital staff.

6. Which of the following is a form of information manipulation?

(a) Re-engineering
(b) Downsizing
(c) Smoothing
(d) Skimming

7. From the point of view of employees, budget slack

(a) helps them achieve the budget by providing a cushion against uncertainty.
(b) is bad because they don't know what to do with it.
(c) is good because it goes into their bonus if it is not used up.
(d) causes them to work harder.

8. Which method of control occurs when employees accommodate themselves to the existing environment by adjusting their expectations and attitudes?

(a) Top-down control
(b) Secondary control
(c) Bottom-up control
(d) Primary control

9. Resistance to ABC/ABM can occur for the following reasons, EXCEPT

(a) employees may not want their superiors to know what they are doing.
(b) an employee's compensation and rewards may be altered.
(c) employees equate ABC/ABM with cost cutting and are afraid of losing their jobs.
(d) employees are worried about losing planned vacation time.

10. Cross-functional teams in today's manufacturing environment:

(a) consist of only design and manufacturing engineers.
(b) consist of only engineers and marketers.
(c) decrease the time for a product to get to market.
(d) increase the time for a product to get to market.

Completion

1. The three schools of managerial thought regarding motivation are ______________ ______________, ______________ ______________, and ______________ ______________.

2. ______________, ______________, and ______________ ______________ are all examples of nongoal-congruent behavior.

3. Information systems designers deal with two interrelated issues: reducing ______________ in information generation, and increasing ______________ among the different parties.

4. As the barriers to various functional areas are being eliminated, employees are increasingly working in ______________-______________ teams.

5. A ______________ ______________ is an individual who takes the initiative and risk to develop a new management accounting and control system.

6. The biggest stumbling block that organizations face in implementing a new MACS is ______________ ______________.

7. ______________ ______________ occurs when employees ask for excess resources above what they need to achieve their organizational goals.

8. ______________ ______________ occurs when employees try to further their own ends by trying to change the existing environment.

9. The hierarchy of ethical principles discussed in the textbook includes ____________, ________________, ________________, ________________, and ________________ rules, norms, or codes of conduct.

10. One element of an effective ethical control system is providing for an ongoing ____________ ____________ of the efficacy of the organization's system.

Problems

1. As a manager at the Rossmane Company you have learned that one of your other managers has been falsifying production reports to include more inventory than has been produced. Given that you have decided to act on the matter, what steps should you follow in dealing with this situation?

2. You are planning to implement an activity-based costing/management system in your organization. One of your colleagues, who has observed another implementation where she used to work, cautions that you might encounter resistance to the change. What kinds of resistance might you encounter and why?

SOLUTIONS TO PRACTICE TEST QUESTIONS AND PROBLEMS

True-False

1. False. The human resources model assumes that individuals have a great deal of knowledge and information to contribute to the organization, and that they are highly creative and responsible. The scientific management school of motivation assumes that people find work objectionable and that they have little creativity to offer on the job.

2. False. The three elements are direction, intensity, and persistence.

3. False. It also requires tailoring for local levels in the organization.

4. True. This statement of ethical responsibilities is essential.

5. False. Ethical dilemmas can be resolved within an organization as well as in court.

6. True. Both types of information are essential in a well-designed MACS.

7. False. Gaming is an example of nongoal-congruent behavior.

8. True. Phase 1 involves designing and building a new MACS, and Phase 2 involves using the new MACS.

9. False. The three general types of cultures are strong functional, strong dysfunctional, and ill-defined.

10. True. The textbook provides many other possible courses of action; resigning and making the issue public is usually not the best course of initial action.

Multiple-Choice

1. d. The three approaches are scientific management, human relations movement, and human resources model. Both Vroom's and Herzberg's theories are models of individual motivation.

2. a. The system should incorporate multiple views, not just top management's.

3. c. While money is one motivator, it is not the primary motivator for many people in the human resources view. To many employees, other factors, such as internal satisfaction and expressing creativity are important motivators.

4. b. A sworn affidavit is not part of an ethical control system.

5. d. Warmth of the hospital staff is a qualitative measure, as one cannot observe or measure it directly, as one could with the amount of output per hour.

6. c. Smoothing is a form of information manipulation.

7. a. Budget slack is built in by employees to provide a cushion or hedge against uncertainty in the work environment.

8. b. Secondary control occurs when employees accommodate themselves to the existing environment by adjusting their expectations and attitudes.

9. d. ABC/ABM is unlikely to affect planned vacation time.

10. c. Cross-functional teams should help decrease time to market because employees in teams can often solve problems more efficiently and effectively, given the benefit of quicker communication and common goals.

Completion

1. scientific management, human relations movement, human resources model

2. Smoothing, gaming, data falsification

3. redundancy, coordination

4. cross functional

5. change champion

6. resistance to change

7. Budget slack

8. Primary control

9. legal, societal, professional, organizational (and/or group), personal

10. internal audit

Problems

1. There are several options. The first is to do nothing and ignore the situation. However, sooner or later your colleague will get caught. If you do nothing, you are also violating the code of ethics, as every employee has a responsibility to report violations of the code.

   Given that you want to do something, it is probably best to start by talking to employees in your organization whose job it is to deal with ethical issues. If no such employees exist or are available, you might start by using a decision model similar to the one described in Table 15.1.

2. Possible reasons for resistance to change are discussed below.

   (a) Employee compensation can be directly affected. As activities are studied and the costs associated with the activities are reassigned, overhead allocations may change in a way that reduces the net income for an employee's division or product line, thereby lowering the bonus or performance evaluation.

   (b) Employees may fear loss of power. An activity analysis could reveal that certain employees are getting credit for the work and accomplishments of others. When the work is reassigned, an employee's sphere of influence could change.

   (c) Many do not want their superiors finding out what they are doing. Employees may be very happy with what they are doing and may anticipate that any change be disruptive to their established routines.

   (d) Employees may associate ABC with cost cutting and job loss. In some cases, the organization may find that it can become more efficient by reorganizing activities. When this occurs, some employees may be let go. Other organizations, however, may commit to reassigning such employees to another position in the organization; this could reduce resistance.

Notes and Questions